THE
WAAF
AT WAR

THE
WAAF
AT WAR

John Frayn Turner

Pen & Sword
AVIATION

First published in Great Britain in 2011 by
PEN & SWORD AVIATION
an imprint of
Pen & Sword Books Limited
47 Church Street
Barnsley
S. Yorkshire S70 2AS

Copyright © John Frayn Turner, 2011

ISBN 978 1 84884 539 8

A CIP catalogue record for this book
is available from the British Library

Typeset in Ehrhardt by Chic Media Ltd

Printed and bound in England
by MPG

Pen & Sword Books Ltd incorporates the imprints of
Pen & Sword Aviation, Pen & Sword Maritime,
Pen & Sword Military,Wharncliffe Local History, Pen & Sword Select,
Pen & Sword Military Classics, Leo Cooper, Remember When,
Seaforth Publishing and Frontline Publishing

For a complete list of Pen & Sword titles please contact:
PEN & SWORD BOOKS LIMITED
47 Church Street, Barnsley, South Yorkshire, S70 2AS, England.
E-mail: enquiries@pen-and-sword.co.uk
Website: www.pen-and-sword.co.uk

Contents

Acknowledgements

I am sincerely grateful to Constance Babington Smith for allowing me to quote her account of the WAAF's part in the battle against the V-weapons. This is from her book *Evidence in Camera*, published by Chatto & Windus. I am also indebted to the following for their help: the head of the Air Historical Branch, Ministry of Defence; the Librarian of the Imperial War Museum; and Audrey Smith. I would like to acknowledge *WAAF with Wings* by YM Lucas (GMS Enterprises, Peterborough). This little book has been very helpful for the chapter on the ferry pilots.

Finally, photo credits. Appreciative thanks are due to the following for photographs, whether for consideration or selection: GMS Enterprises (*WAAF with Wings* by YM Lucas); Sutton Publishing (*Our Wartime Days* by Squadron Leader Beryl E Escott); Patrick Stephen Ltd (*Women in Air Force Blue* by Squadron Leader Beryl E Escott); Ministry of Defence; Her Majesty's Stationery Office; RAF Museum; RSRE Malvern; Air Historical Branch, Ministry of Defence; RAF Halton; This England.

Introduction

How the WAAF was Born

No one knew it then, but the First World War was in its final year. On 1 April 1918, the Royal Air Force was formed by the merger of the Royal Naval Air Service and the Royal Flying Corps. And on the same day, the Women's Royal Air Force emerged from the Women's Royal Naval Service and Queen Mary's Army Auxiliary Corps, both already attached to flying units of their respective Service to release airmen for more active duties.

By autumn 1918, the WRAF had expanded dramatically, while reports from the Front in France became better each day. People were talking about the end of the war, though this had been heard too often to be taken seriously. Then suddenly the news of the Armistice came as a stupendous surprise. Peace returned at the eleventh hour of the eleventh day of the eleventh month.

Altogether, 556 officers and 31,764 women passed in and out of the WRAF. Women went to work on a remarkable number of RAF trades. Besides the normal clerical branch, girls served in technical trades from acetylene welding to mending balloon silk. In the clerical branch, the WRAF only enrolled girls as shorthand typists if they had trained for the job in civilian life. RAF pay offices were glad of girls for bookkeeping, while the WRAF also took over as stores clerks. As early as 1918, with the war still in progress, many RAF telephone switchboards were run by women, who sometimes also operated as telegraphists.

Next to the clerical branch, the largest was the domestic or household branch. WRAFs enrolled in their hundreds as cooks, mess orderlies and general domestics. Many of the girls had the advantage of having cooked at large houses in the pre-war era of cheap labour for servants. As well as orderlies, WRAFs also worked as laundresses.

But it was on the 'flight' side that girls really shone and showed their technical abilities. They were trained as carpenters, sail makers, dopers, painters, riggers and salvage workers. In this war, new planes came in crates from the factories to be assembled on the spot: an early example of do-it-yourself. In the carpenters' shops they worked on the wings, propellers and struts of the biplanes, making the frames later. As riggers, too, WRAFs acquired a real reputation and came as close as women were likely to get to the actual business of war in the air.

The RAF also trusted the girls to be trained as engine fitters, while more feminine in character was the work of women in the sail makers' shop. Their sewing machines seemed strange appliances for helping to build aeroplanes, but they did, in fact, cut out, stitch and machine the fabric for the main planes, tail planes and ailerons. After assembly of these model-aircraft-like machines, the dopers took over. In most RAF stations, girls entirely operated the dope shop, where there was always a strong smell of pear drops. WRAFs saw that the planes were tautened by a first coat of dope, while another one gave the machines extra strength. Finally, tape bindings were doped on to aircraft frameworks.

The girls of the WRAF also grew proficient in paint shops, adorning wings and fuselage with the familiar red, white and blue roundels. In technical stores, women replaced and released men. And so to the pigeon women! The WRAF became responsible for the pigeons taken up in airships to fly to base with messages. At airship stations around the coast, WRAFs helped to form landing parties for airships. In bad weather, all the WRAF was called out to help the landing party, or when an especially large airship was due. On one stormy Sunday a coastal patrol airship came in quite unexpectedly and all WRAF ranks including the cooks had to help. Afterwards the cooks had to hurry back to finish preparing the Station's Sunday dinner. Even in those far-off days, the girls wore trousers when working as fitters or on other technical jobs.

Biggin Hill, immortalized over twenty years later, was a wireless experimental station and one of the few employing WRAF officers on technical work. They acquitted themselves with distinction on experimental duties in connection with wireless telegraphy and telephony, as well as in the test department. Another link with later events in the Second World War was the London Photo Centre, where seventy women did the developing, printing, retouching and enlarging of aerial photos, including negatives of sectors of the battlefields. They also handled photos of all the types of aeroplanes, seaplanes and airships.

Of course, WRAFs could not foresee then that link with the WAAFs of the 1940s on the flying bomb and aerial reconnaissance interpretation. Meanwhile, after the First World War, WRAF recruiting was naturally reduced and eventually the Service was disbanded.

Under two decades later, however, war clouds were lowering and looming once more, and in Douglas Bader's words 'Hitler's shadow was long over Europe.' On 28 June 1939 the WAAF was born. It then had just 1,734 members serving under the umbrella of the Royal Air Force companies of the Auxiliary Territorial Service. Their six kinds of duties seemed very similar to those of the original WAAF: cooks, clerks, mess orderlies, Military Transport (MT) drivers, equipment assistants and fabric workers (on Balloon Squadrons).

As September started, Germany was invading Poland and refusing to withdraw. Just after 11am on Sunday 3 September, the British Prime Minister Neville Chamberlain spoke these historic words: 'Consequently, this country is at war with Germany ...'

At that time, Britain was still seriously under-armed. In the air, the RAF would rely on the Spitfire and Hurricane fighters, but in September 1938 at the time of the Munich crisis just five squadrons had received Hurricanes, while deliveries of Spitfires were only just starting. From the point of view of Britain's air power, the extra respite given by Mr Chamberlain's appeasement of Hitler at Munich was crucial. The intervening year enabled the RAF to double its Fighter Command strength. From the total of nearly 500 Hurricanes delivered to squadrons and to the reserve, some three-quarters had been built in that vital year. When war started, eighteen squadrons were equipped with Hurricanes. There were then 400 Spitfires already in service and over 2,000 on order. But Britain was still short of fighters, pilots to fly them and ground personnel of both sexes.

The first few months were dubbed 'The Phoney War' which was, in fact, far from the truth. The RAF and WAAF were expanding steadily. Then in mid–May 1940 the German juggernaut thundered through the Low Countries. Within a week, the British Expeditionary Force was in drastic danger. On 21 May, the War Office was considering emergency evacuation of very large forces.

Throughout the week the now-immortal small ships and smaller-still boats assembled around the south coasts, while over in Belgium four divisions of the BEF were in imminent danger of encirclement near Lille. Then on Sunday 26 May the order was given to implement Operation DYNAMO. It was estimated that the enemy would reach the coast in two days, but for some reason they headed away from the retreating troops, giving them an extra week before the all-out attack. The result was the historic evacuation of Dunkirk. The Battle for France was over. The Battle of Britain was about to begin …

Chapter 1

The Battle of Britain

Before the Battle of Britain really began, WAAF Corporal Joan Pearson was posted to the Fighter Command station of Detling. The air was in her blood and she had been learning to fly herself before the war. Now she was doing the next best thing by helping the RAF in the spring of 1940.

The WAAF quarters were near the airfield and the girls heard planes taking off during the evening of 30 May 1940 – the week of Dunkirk. Joan was off duty and went to bed as usual that night. She dozed into a fitful sleep soon after midnight. It was hard to sleep soundly as planes were continually revving up; patrols going out or returning. Being in the medical branch, she was always on the alert, even when off duty. It was instinctive.

About 1am, Joan awoke at the approach of a plane. One engine had cut out; she could tell that at once. Before she could do anything except sit up in bed, she heard a reverberating, rending crash followed by an uncanny second's silence. The engines started to roar.

The aircraft had crash-landed near the WAAF quarters. By then her duty trousers and fisherman's jersey were on, and she was groping her way out of the hut. She could not remember if she had put on gumboots or shoes. All she knew was that here she was, running over the wet, dewy grass and across the cement road, stumbling toward the guardhouse. A few flames were moving in the air and there must have been the noise of the crash.

A twinkling light – that meant the ambulance. She must warn the guard to undo the gates and be ready to let it through. The guard grunted as she ran by him. He knew her, and she shouted to him: 'The ambulance is behind.'

She kept running hard towards the crash and came to an RAF policeman. 'You can't go over there,' he yelled, trying to stop her climbing the fence. But she could and did. Men were shouting for the doctor and the ambulance.

Joan yelled: 'Coming!'

A fire crackled from the crash. The nettles stung her in the ditch on the far side of the fence. She was near the scene now. A figure panted up and she saw another one silhouetted against the flames. A man tried to drag at a person in the plane. Joan told him: 'Go and get the fence down for the ambulance.'

She knew there were bombs aboard the burning aircraft, which must explode soon, yet she struggled to drag the pilot – seriously hurt by the crash – free from the flames. He was groaning, so she decided to render first aid on the spot, in case of further damage. Another officer had been killed outright.

She fought her way through the wreckage, stood on it and roused the stunned pilot. Somehow, in the holocaust of heat, she stripped off his parachute harness and found that his neck was hurting. 'Keep clear,' he gasped weakly at her, thinking of the bombs. But she stayed with him and helped him out of his cockpit.

It was then that the petrol tanks blew. Joan lay down quickly and tried to shield the light from the pilot's face, as he was suffering from severe shock and was only semi-conscious. Somehow again she got him completely clear of the aircraft, to about thirty yards off, and was holding his head carefully to prevent further dislocation or injury. She had the bombs at the back of her mind.

It was then that a 120-pounder erupted. Instinctively she hurled herself on top of the pilot to protect him from the blast and splinters. There was one more bomb still to go. Meanwhile, Joan continued to comfort him. He was conscious now and most concerned about a small cut on his lip in case it showed. A man crawled up and lent Joan his handkerchief to tend the pilot while she waited for the ambulance to arrive. The bomb seemed to have taken all the oxygen out of the air.

Joan knew it must be a matter of only seconds before the other bomb went up, so she ran to the fence to help the medical officer over with the stretcher. The pilot would soon be safe and in a few moments they got aboard the ambulance, still in the middle of the May night.

They were just in time, for the second bomb burst with an earth-quaking explosion. More blast and more splinters. But they were safely tucked in the vehicle and on their way to the sick quarters. Joan went straight on duty to see to the pilot's wounds herself, finishing for the night about 3am. Sick parade was at 8.30am next morning, as usual. And she was there – as usual.

On 18 July 1940 Assistant Section Officer, no longer Corporal, Joan Pearson read her award of the Empire Gallantry Medal, later to be converted into the George Cross.

With the Battle of Britain came the deluge from the skies. Detling seemed to breed bravery, for one of the six WAAF girls to win the Military Medal received it for her behaviour there during an air raid. She was Corporal Josephine Maude Gwynne Robins.

As the Luftwaffe was attacking this valuable fighter station, Josephine was in a dugout listening to the crescendo overhead. Then a bomb suddenly struck the shelter. Several of the RAF men in the dugout died instantly. Two more were badly hurt by the blast. Though dust and fumes filled the crumbled shelter, Josephine at once staggered her way to the wounded and did what she could for them. As the dust began to settle, she helped get them out of the demolished dugout and then ran for a stretcher. After she had fetched it, she stayed with the wounded men until they could be evacuated from the area. All the time, Josephine displayed courage and coolness amid a fierce air raid, which caused casualties not only to men but to the WAAF as well.

Now the Battle of Britain was really on, and two more Military Medals were soon won by WAAF girls. In August 1940, nineteen-year-old Sergeant Jean Mary Youle, from Weybridge, was on duty in the telephone exchange when the station – one of the Army Co-operation Command – was bombed by five enemy aircraft. Then the bombs got nearer and nearer until the building containing the exchange received the shattering sound of a direct hit.

'We had a warning,' Jean said, 'and later heard the bombs

exploding around us in an attack lasting about five minutes – five rotten minutes. I was standing at the exchange at the time and tried to discover which of our telephone lines were put out of order as a result of the damage. One bomb fell some twenty yards from me and others dropped fifty or sixty yards off. I was neither hurt nor stunned – though debris was scattered. Two other girls with me in the exchange also continued working and the broken lines were in operation again as soon as possible.'

What Jean did not stress was that the staff was subjected to a stream of bomb splinters as well as the inevitable plaster. It was solely due to her example that the telephone operators carried on with their vital task throughout the raid.

It was still August 1940, when Goering had boasted he would be in London, and the third Military Medal went to twenty-four-year-old Corporal Joan Avis Hearn for her reaction to a similar situation to that of Jean Youle's. She was at her telephone one night during that fateful month when an air raid developed and a number of bombs began to fall on her observation unit. Damage was extensive, and then several heavier bombs burst alongside the block where Joan was working alone controlling her telephones. The sudden sound was overpowering. All the windows of her block were blown in. Glass split and splintered over the floors. Heavy walls cracked and threatened to collapse. One of the main walls of two rooms had a jagged rent right down it and looked like caving in at any minute. But amid all the din and danger, Joan never moved an inch from her instruments. Steadily she reported the course of the enemy bombers over the phones, realizing how much the RAF fighters and ack-ack gunners were depending on her work.

She went on telephoning the result of plots coolly, accurately, and in one of the most dramatic messages ever sent by a woman at war, she said: 'The course of the enemy bombers is only too apparent to me because the bombs are almost dropping on my head.'

Three more Military Medals were to be won by the WAAF, all of them in the Battle of Britain, and all at that most famous fighter station of all, Biggin Hill. Constantly in the thickest of the battle, the

WAAFs there won not only the MMs but an MBE as well.

Towards the end of August, the very first heavy air raid on the station did only slight damage to the actual buildings, though high explosives and delayed-action bombs ripped up the ground around the vital runways in a fanatical attempt to stop the Spitfires and Hurricanes taking off. Twenty-eight-year-old Sergeant Joan Eugene Mortimer was on duty in the station armoury during the raid. Though stacks of ammunition lay stored near her office, just asking to be ignited, she manned the telephone, passing instructions to the various defence posts around the airfield.

As the raid got worse, she went on with her job and also managed to shout encouragement above the din to airmen in the same building as her. If any of them had had doubts about women at war, they never would again. At last the raid was over, but the tall, slim girl from Yorkshire with blue eyes and brown hair had not finished what she considered as her duties.

She went outside the Biggin Hill buildings and walking amid the smouldering aftermath of an air raid she calmly pegged out with red flags all the places on the aerodrome where unexploded bombs lay buried. Then asked about her actions and her future, she said simply: 'Naturally I want to stay here and continue my work.'

That was MM number one for Biggin Hill. Before the other two were won, in the following month, a massive enemy onslaught one afternoon at teatime presaged a whole series of raids that pulverized the station.

Assistant Section Officer Felicity Hanbury won the MBE for her part in the first and following raids. At the start of the first, she and two other WAAF officers, together with some RAF men, went to the nearest trench. The steady sound of patrolling aircraft overhead turned to the zoom and roar of dogfights. Bombs straddled the airfield, getting alarmingly louder as they came closer. The thundering grew so loud that Felicity clutched her ears. She thought they would burst otherwise. Bombs were dropping all around them now, and above the noise they could hear the dogfights making an amazing din.

One bomb fell a few feet from the entrance to their shelter. Stones and earth flew inside, and a blast of hot air pushed them sideways across the trench. Another bomb dropped near, and again the shuddering noise of engines, ack-ack guns, bombs and machine guns made Felicity feel as though she were falling to bits.

It was all over in ten minutes. Then came a lull, and they heard the throb of their aircraft returning to refuel and rearm. A messenger came to get the padre and another officer, as a trench had been hit at the far end of the aerodrome. Felicity went quickly to the airwomen's trenches by the guardroom. No one knew if they were alright. On her way past craters and debris, she saw her first dead person – a NAAFI girl lying in the hedge. Then she found that one of the airwomen's trenches had got a direct hit and the airwomen were buried underneath. The station officer came along at that moment and said they must get some volunteers to dig the girls out.

There was another trench at the other end of a horseshoe of houses. Felicity went to see the airwomen in it and told them they could come out. A corporal ran off to get blankets. A bomb had blown in the end of the first trench, cutting off the entrance and killing a sick-quarter attendant. The wounded were got out, laid on stretchers in the hedges, and they coped with the worst. Some went to sick quarters, others to hospital. Several had broken legs and arms. There was a stream of ambulance traffic towards the nearest hospital for hours after the raid.

In that trench shelter where the sick-quarter attendant was killed, Flight Sergeant Gartside's mind went blank after the bomb burst. The girls said she was conscious and issued orders as usual. She made them all laugh for a minute by trying to sit up after the shock and saying: 'Heavens, I've broken my back,' and then almost in the same breath: 'Heavens, I've broken my teeth, too.' The girls laughed so much that they did not worry any more till the soldiers asked if anyone were alive down there.

When medical help came, the flight sergeant said: 'Look after the others. Don't worry about me. I'm all right.' Flight Sergeant Gartside had actually broken her back and spent some weeks lying on it in plaster, before recovering enough to be invalided out of the WAAF.

Some WAAF quarters had been hit, but they salvaged what they could and put the airwomen inside. Felicity thought the cooks particularly were magnificent. The airmen's cookhouse was one of the few buildings that had not been hit. It was at the end of the aerodrome. The army ground defence and airmen were all fed from the WAAF cookhouse for some days. The WAAF cooks were frying sausages and mash for the men till long after midnight that first night. Felicity took hurricane lamps along, as the electric light had gone, and then she collected some food to take to the WAAF plotters on duty.

A bomb had fallen plumb in the middle of the road and burst the gas, electric light and water mains. The heat and dust were terrific. The girls stacked up the dirty plates, and later tanks came along and kept the cookhouse supplied with water.

The WAAF officers slept in the CO's mess that night, as there was a delayed-action bomb in front of their mess. Felicity went to bed about 2am, as there did not seem anything else to do. But she did not sleep much for delayed-action bombs kept going off and enemy aircraft were overhead all night dropping flares. A cow kept mooing in the field opposite, and she was sure it had been hit. Then there was an alarm at 8.30 the next morning. The station broadcast was out of action, so two buglers stood outside the Operations Room and bugled like mad. They went down the trenches, but the enemy was driven off. The raiders came again at 10am, when Felicity was in the cookhouse, and one heard the zoom of the dogfights once more, mingled with the whistling of bombs. But it did not sound very serious, and they joked in the trenches and were soon back at work. Another raid followed in the afternoon, when the Operation Room's roof fell on the WAAF plotters, who were dug out without harm. These attacks on Biggin Hill continued for several days.

In May 1941 Flight Officer Felicity Hanbury left Buckingham Palace with her MBE. Later she became Director of the WRAF and in 1949 was made a Dame Commander of the Order of the British Empire.

But back to September 1940 now, and the climax of the Battle of Britain. The Germans were trying to neutralize Biggin Hill, but with WAAFs like Corporal Elspeth Henderson and Sergeant Helen Turner they never would. Elspeth Henderson, of Edinburgh, was small and auburn haired. Before the war she travelled a great deal and lived abroad, some of the time in Ceylon. She spoke fluent French and German, and had been secretary to a surgeon. Helen Turner, of Holloway, London, was among the early women recruits who worked with the Air Force in the First World War, and joined in the days of the RFC. She completed four years' service. Then for ten years she was a telephone operator at the Savoy Hotel and after that served seven years in a similar job with a big advertising agency.

When enemy bombers throbbed once more over Biggin Hill on a particular day in September, the two WAAF girls were both on duty, Elspeth in charge of a special telephone line and Helen as the switchboard operator. Bombs began falling perilously near to their building, but both of them went on with their jobs, although they knew that there was only a light roof over their heads. Then came a direct hit. Neither of them was hurt and they still carried on with their work. 'There was nothing much else we could do, anyway, was there?' Elspeth asked afterwards. Then the building caught fire, and the flames spurted and spat across the room. At last they were ordered to leave.

'When we did leave,' said Helen, 'we had to crawl out through the wreckage, crawling through the broken-down walls to safety. I felt a bit sorry for some of the youngsters in the building at the time because it was their first experience of bombs. I did my best to cheer them up.'

Elspeth Henderson and Helen Turner were awarded the Military Medal at the same time as Joan Mortimer. The Commanding Officer of the station said of them: 'These three girls have shown amazing pluck in carrying on their work under the strain of falling bombs. I am proud to have them working on this station. There is no doubt that their example during two days of bombing inspired all around them.'

Meanwhile, the Luftwaffe was dropping load after load of bombs on other Fighter Command stations too, but the WAAFs took it all. Here is what happened at two typical stations, told by the girls who lived through it.

Aircraftwoman Cooper was at North Weald on 25 August 1940.

'It was very hot; we were waiting to go on watch at 4pm when we heard the warning on the tannoy. As we were hurrying to the shelters, we looked up and saw the enemy planes glinting in the sun and getting into formation, ready to do a run across the station. We were just down when the first bomb, a screaming one, fell near.

'There were not more than six WAAF and three RAF in our shelter. When the first bomb fell, we all involuntarily sat forward with our hands over our heads. I think we heard the second bomb. After that it was just a roar. All the corrugated iron of the shelter cracked. There was an incredible smell of explosives and the heat of the blast, which swept through the shelter. The escape hatch had been blown off the hinges, and I shall never forget the smell of the heat.

'We didn't know when the raid was over. Eventually one of the men put his head out of the trench and heard firing. But soon it stopped. We found afterwards that the tannoy had been blown out of action.

'My first thought was then of the Ops Block. We were due to go on duty at 4pm, and it was almost that then. When we looked out there was a horrible sight. It's best forgotten. They'd hit a crowded trench quite near. In the next trench to ours, some RAF were taking a boy out with his shoulder off, and another who'd lost a leg. Two plotters who had been in that trench were helping.

'The first bomb had fallen within ten feet of the mouth of our trench and blown up the concrete road between the trench and the WAAF quarters. As we were below ground level, we were all right.

'A WAAF sick-quarter attendant had a bad time. She'd just left the sick quarters when she saw it blow up behind her. She stared into a trench crying: "It's all right, I'm safe" and found she was alone. She stayed put till the end of the raid. Then she went out and as she was crossing the grass a delayed action bomb went off. But she reached what remained of the sick quarters safely.

'We left the trenches and went first into our quarters where we found the beds riddled with bullets. We'd only got up a short time before. All the glass was out of the windows, and they'd machine-gunned the rooms.

'On the way to Ops Block we met the CO, Wing Commander

Beamish, busy worrying about the water mains. He'd been up in the thick of it during the battle.

'We then took over in the Ops Room and the business of getting information through to Group were done by the WAAF. The lights and telephones were gone, and it looked like the black hole of Calcutta by candlelight. Operators from this station had never stopped for a minute, and we were all anticipating another attack.

'We worked in Emergency Ops all through the night. It was the first time we had been allowed on at night. Apparently they thought it would be too much of a strain. We couldn't go back to our quarters for a week. There were DA bombs in the gardens, and one had actually landed on my long-cherished cabbage patch. We slept on floors anywhere we could find room. We had to carry water in buckets for 200 yards for washing up and everything else. A serious concern was our makeup, which we couldn't get. So we all bought powder and stuff at the NAAFI and carried our face around with us in the pocket of our gas masks. Then everyone wondered how we managed to look so smart and clean.

'We had just got back to our quarters to get our things and were allowed in one at a time so as not to disturb the DA bombs (we were sleeping then in the Barrack Blocks) when the station had its second attack. That was 3 September at 10.45am. We sat in trenches for about ten minutes while we heard a running commentary on the tannoy. We had time then to be frightened. Hardly any of us hoped to get out alive.

'There was one WAAF in the trench who hadn't been on the station for the first raid. She insisted on staying at the entrance to see what happened. But at the first bomb she came down with a rush.

'I sat on the bench and there was one plotter beside me and two others standing in front; and we all gripped each other. It seemed a much longer raid. They used HEs, anti-personnel bombs, which just touch the ground and explode with a terrific blast, and incendiaries.

'After the bombing we heard machine-guns firing off and thought they had got the ammunition dump. The decontamination centre proved to be far from bombproof. The MT yard was ablaze. The Ops Block had been hit, but not much damage was done. There was a DA bomb outside the telephone exchange. In fact, except the officers' mess, which survived bomb raids, there was hardly any building that hadn't been damaged. They got some of the hangars, but all our aircraft, of course, were up, except a few, which were being serviced.

'Two other plotters and I climbed into a civilian lorry and went off to Emergency Ops. All the service transport in the yard had been blown up. On the way we thought there was another attack coming, but it was only our aircraft returning.

'We ran Ops from Emergency Ops and worked all that day and through the next night. We had to cook for ourselves and the airmen.'

On the very same day, 3 September 1940, the first anniversary of the outbreak of war, Section Officer Yates (née Petters) was at Debden Fighter Command station in Cambridgeshire. She takes up the story of the WAAFs under fire.

'On September 3, about 2 o'clock, the siren sounded. Before everyone had got inside the trenches – about 15 seconds after the warning – there were the most ear-splitting rumbles and bangs. I was just entering my trench when suddenly I found myself lying on the floorboards, having been hurled down four steps into the pitch blackness. The noise was so deafening and terrifying that our whole lives passed before us in a few seconds, which we certainly thought to be our last. Pieces of the trench fell upon us and my tin hat was knocked off. The bombing ceased and all we heard in the deathly stillness of the trench was the whine of diving aircraft and splutter of machine guns and the roar of our squadrons taking off. Then we smelt burning.

'Before we had time to utter a word or contemplate further, I heard a man's shout: "Come out of the trench! There's an unexploded bomb on top!" and the girls' cry: "It's on fire this end!" Out we filed and ran to the nearest trench, to find it full, and then to the next with no luck; so we had to throw ourselves on the ground.

'As we emerged from the trench, I thought immediately, this is like the film *Things to Come*. The buildings around us were damaged and many knocked down. Dust and smoke were in the air, and there was a solid ring of craters around us. Afterwards we counted fifty within fifty yards of our two trenches, and an enormous one just outside the entrance to our shelter.

'Then the all clear sounded, and for the next hour a voice came over the tannoy giving instructions. These were mostly about the positions of unexploded bombs, and where not to go. As one had to skirt the bombs by a range of twenty-five yards, it was very difficult to pick a route to anywhere. The playing field was the only safe place, so the airwomen were assembled there and the roll-call taken, to find – by a miraculous piece of luck – that all were present, and only a few slightly injured, bruised, or cut by flying glass.

'Some WAAF drivers were caught in the MT yards, so dived under their vehicles. When they emerged, they found three large craters in the centre of the yard.

'One WAAF was washing her hair, and before she could remove the soap from her eyes and run to a trench, she had ceiling plaster falling about her, so dived under the kitchen table. Those in Ops carried on with complete coolness although the lights went out, and telephones to the squadrons failed.

'After the roll call, a job was found for most people. We discovered that the complete street where the airwomen were quartered was out of bounds. At least half the houses were unsafe, and unexploded bombs were around them. Many who had been off duty in their quarters came out in all states of undress – slacks, overalls, and some even in underwear – with only a coat or mac thrown over their shoulders. They couldn't get their clothes for several days.'

HM The Queen paid her own tribute to the bravery of the WAAF when she visited a station of Fighter Command soon after the Battle of Britain had been won. She said to the senior WAAF officer of about 2,000 girls attached to similar fighter stations throughout southeast England: 'I hear that your women are magnificent.'

'Thank you, Your Majesty,' replied the WAAF squadron officer. 'Yes – magnificent is the best word for them.'

The squadron officer had a file of heroism displayed by WAAFs at various fighter stations – many girls besides those already mentioned. There was the case of the squadron leader in charge of the administration side of one station who owed his legs and probably his life to a single WAAF. He had been about to enter a shelter near the airfield when a bomb fell, badly wounding him in the legs. The WAAF, a nurse before the war, ran over to him as he lay there helpless. The squadron leader was losing blood very fast from the wounds, but she immediately improvised a tourniquet and stopped the flow. The raid went on, and bombs continued to fall very close to them, but she helped a station medical officer to take the injured officer over to sick quarters. Then the raid did eventually end, and it was safe to move about again, the squadron leader was removed to hospital, where the doctors declared quite definitely that the girl's prompt action had saved his legs from having to be amputated.

In view of the record of gallantry by WAAFs throughout the Battle of Britain, it was scarcely surprising, therefore, when listeners to a BBC broadcast by an RAF officer heard how he had become 'a converted man' in favour of the WAAF. This is how he explained his conversion:

'About six months ago, I tried to tell you something of how the fighter pilots of my station had fought and helped to win the Battle of Britain. Much has happened since. Every day now we are going for the Hun in the Battle of France – but that's another story that's only just beginning.

'In that last talk, I very much wanted to say something about the Women's Auxiliary Air Force, because they helped us out more than most people appreciate. I should like to do it now.

'In the first place, I ought to say that I am a converted man. As an officer of some twenty-six years' service, I sincerely believed that war was a job for men, that in war women could tackle the more quiet and comfortable civilian jobs and leave it to fathers, brothers, and cousins to fill the fighting services.

'Then at the beginning of this war came the news that we – the Royal Air Force – were to have women. Women in our operations rooms, women driving our transport, manning our signals and our teleprinters, even invading our messes. Petticoats in the RAF.

'When the first little trickle of WAAFs drifted into my station, I was inwardly rather resentful, slightly amused, believing that it could not last; that it might be pretty-pretty during the quiet days, but when the going got tough the folly of it would be seen.

'How wrong I was.

'Long before the respite came in November, I had cause to thank goodness that this country could produce such a race of women as the WAAFs on my station. Let me give you an example. In the daylight mass bombing in August and September of last year, in a flimsy building on the aerodrome, I saw my WAAF plotters, with their earphones pressed to their ears to keep out the inferno of noise from the torrent of bombs that were bursting all around, steady and calm at their posts – plotting. Not a murmur or movement from a single one of them, though the building was literally rocking and each one knew that she and the building might be airborne at any moment. But that was last year – those buildings are now no longer in the target area.

'When I look back, how stupid I was to resent that first intrusion of WAAFs, but I didn't know then what I know now; those men I valued were wanted for work elsewhere, for work more fitted to a man. That first little trickle of WAAFs was a sign of strength, not weakness – it meant expansion. From that moment onwards, I welcomed every succeeding batch of airwomen to my station, as I know every commanding officer does today with good reason, for it means more and more men released to form more and more squadrons to fight the Hun – yet the same efficiency is maintained and often increased. As month succeeds month, I hope to see the thousands more we need come in to give us a hand to fight the Battle of Europe.

'Last year was the proudest and happiest of my life, in command of a fighter station. I venture to say – and I hope they are listening – that last year was also one of the happiest years in the young lives of many WAAFs who served there with me. But then you can't help being happy on an Air Force station – at least I find it so. There's so much to do, to see; a thrill a day.

'The Royal Air Force is proud of its WAAFs – each one of them does the work of one man, and does it darned well. They helped us to win the Battle of Britain in ever-increasing numbers. I hope to see them come in to give us a hand in winning the Battle of Europe.'

Chapter 2

The Blitz

Hellfire – or Shellfire – Corner: that was Dover in the Battle of Britain. And for four more years it remained right in the front line. The WAAF was there all the time. As members of the Dover Balloon Barrage, in fact, a small group of them stayed nearer to the enemy than any other girls in the women's services. On a clear day, they could see across those twenty miles that had meant the difference between defeat and Dunkirk. And on these days, they looked through a telescope and actually spotted German soldiers on sentry duty along the French coast. No one could be closer than that!

Innumerable times they sustained enemy air attack. And just as often, when the long-range German guns opened up from the other side of the Channel, the shells never burst far away. But the WAAFs were unperturbed. They just got used to it, that was all.

Once during the course of an hour, some fifty shells from the Germans fell in the Dover area, causing casualties and damage at 961 Balloon Barrage Headquarters. The medical officer was among those killed. Leading Aircraftwoman Kathleen Lucy McKinlay, a motor driver, was wounded in the right hand and left thigh, but she acted as an ambulance driver and succeeded in removing all the other casualties. Not only was she in teeth-gritting pain, but also had to make several journeys under the continuing shellfire to an EMS hospital a mile or two away. It was only when the shellfire had finished and all casualties had received attention that Kathleen could be persuaded to have her own injuries attended. She won the British Empire Medal.

In charge of these airwomen around the Dover defences was a WAAF officer whose task was to look after their welfare. Every time the siren sounded – and that was up to a dozen times a day – she made the round exposed to whatever danger was on its way. To the cookhouse she went, where WAAF cooks were preparing meals for the RAF; to the messing stores where WAAF messing orderlies were packing food and supplies to take round to the many dispersed barrage balloon sites guarding the coast; to the nursing orderlies, standing ready with their first aid outfits; to the clerks, the equipment assistants, and perhaps most important of all, to the telephonists. For no matter how near the shells and bombs burst, they had to keep the lines of communication open, for this was war.

When the shelling or bombing got dangerously near, airwomen who could leave their posts went into a shelter about twenty yards from squadron headquarters. Across that distance – less than the length of a cricket pitch but seeming so much more – the WAAF officer made frequent trips to see that there were no casualties among her girls still on duty. After a raid, she often quietly congratulated herself on her good fortune, when she saw shrapnel strewn along her path. It was all so much a matter of luck, this chance between life and death.

The German long-range guns went on firing and their planes went on coming. Working in exposed buildings on the edge of the Channel cliffs, the 200 airwomen did not fail. Another particular case came one night when a salvo of eight shells landed in a compound and destroyed every building except the part of the operational block in which a section of WAAF were working. All electricity was cut off through the action and for seven hours the girls worked by candlelight.

At times there were casualties, fatal and otherwise, among the personnel. But the CO reported that he did not receive a single request for a posting to a less dangerous spot. Moreover, when the strain was at its most intense, and he felt that the girls should be given a rest, his offer to permit one section to have a forty-eight-hour pass was refused until their work was less urgent and the privilege could be extended to everyone on the station.

During many of the heaviest bombardments, Leading Aircraftwoman Beryl Starkey of Warrington, Elizabeth Davies of

Ashford, Kent and Dorothy Wynne of Doncaster, transport drivers, were called on to convey personnel to and from sleeping quarters by night. Their route lay between our own long-range batteries, which were replying to the enemy guns, and the area in which enemy shells were falling. They did this duty by timing the salvoes, which usually fell at intervals of seven minutes.

In their off-duty time, this little band of airwomen found plenty to do – shows, pictures and dances. But if the siren sounded, with its wailing warning of imminent shelling or bombing, they had to return to their duty posts, like any man on active service. The warning of these attacks could be measured in tens of seconds rather than minutes. Loudspeakers all over the town announced the call to girls in Dover to return to base.

The girls did not always avail themselves of the diversions offered as a relief from the constant strain of bombardment. Instead, they had sewing bees, when they all gathered together to make home comforts for the RAF on dispersed balloon sites. These men were many miles from any towns. The men's standard setting consisted of one hut and a cookhouse, shared by all the crew who made up each bleak, isolated outpost. They certainly needed comforts, and as many homely things as possible, so at the Balloon Squadron Headquarters, the girls got busy.

One item that the girls designed gave the men special delight was a quantity of tea cloths, with the number of the particular balloon site stitched on each one. The girls made these as a surprise and put them on the Christmas tree for the balloon men. Washing up became almost a pride and pleasure. Meals were certainly one of the only other pleasures there. Gloves, socks and pullovers also occupied a lot of the girls' time, as these comforts against the winter were always in greater demand than they could meet.

The girls did get away from camp sometimes, and on their twenty-four-hour passes off duty, people outside Dover welcomed them. All the WAAFs had their 'foster homes', which meant a lot to girls a long way from their real ones. At these houses, out of range of the heavy guns at least, they often spent a well-earned day's rest.

Through the years at Dover, the morale remained amazingly

high. Cheerfully every morning, the WAAFs changed the emergency water supply, always kept ready in large closed-in tins. Emergencies became almost normal, in fact, and the way of life assumed a state of accepted tension.

When asked which she found the more trying of the two types of attack on the Dover area, one airwoman answered: 'Well, I would rather have the bombing. Shells seem so uncanny as they seem to arrive out of the blue.' Which, of course, was just what they did.

Throughout the country, too, the WAAFs were having a tough time in the Blitz, but like the front-line girls at Dover, they rose to whatever was required of them. Often it happened unexpectedly, as in the lounge of an RAF convalescent home one morning in 1942, when WAAF waitresses were handing round elevenses to pilots recuperating and to the medical staff. Then the level of laughter and chatter dried up suddenly. They heard the unmistakable throb of enemy aircraft overhead, unusually low and menacing.

With a thin, whining whistle, the bomb came. Glass smashed; masonry crumbled. Recovering with an effort from the shock of the eruption, the men and women in the lounge struggled through still-swirling dust and the wreckage towards the centre of the direct hit. Within a few minutes, RAF medical officers, nursing sisters and VADs (Voluntary Aid Detachment) had converted the dining room of the convalescent home into an emergency dressing station where WAAF clerks and orderlies worked under their direction.

The bomb had hit the gas main, but WAAF cooks were heating water on the kitchen ranges as quickly as they could, and waitresses rushed it up to the dressing station to help treat the first wounded. The WAAF telephonists stayed at their posts throughout the incident, working ceaselessly calling extra ambulances and other local aid. Under the orders of the WAAF administrative officer, messing staff and nursing orderlies who had escaped serious injury were mustered and found useful jobs. One girl had her injured arm stitched, sat quietly for a few minutes, and then disappeared. Later they found her sweeping away the glass in the hallway through which the stretchers had to be carried. 'I might as well use my good arm, anyhow,' she said.

A VAD and another WAAF had been busy in a patient's room when the bomb burst. They were shot out to the terrace below and buried among the wreckage. After about half an hour, the two women, badly bruised and cut, managed to free themselves. They thought of their patient, whom they found buried deeper and pinned beneath a beam. They tore away at the debris until they had freed his head and shoulders, with a great strain, and while the VAD hurried for help, the WAAF stayed to support him as well as she could. The moment she was relieved, she went to help other casualties, and there were plenty.

Two WAAF nursing orderlies were with an RAF patient in one of the upstairs rooms. The blast flung them to the floor. This broke the patient's leg. The nurses found that they could not get out of the room for help at once, so working as a perfect team, they put the injured leg in a splint. Conveniently at hand, this splint was part of the wreckage in the room! Later, when helpers broke through and brought the casualty downstairs, the RAF medical officer praised the two girls for their efficiency and presence of mind.

This same characteristic efficiency produced hot soup and sandwiches in under the hour: lunch at lunchtime, despite a direct hit. The WAAF catering officer had reason to be proud of her cooks and waitresses, who all day long supplied the food and stimulants needed to meet the situation.

Late afternoon found the RAF and WAAF clerks and equipment assistant dealing with the records and clothing of evacuated patients, and collected scattered personal possessions and gear. When the medical officers, RAF nursing sisters and VADs had time to pause, they picked their way in ones and twos trough the rubble and damage, where an evening meal awaited them. They were understandably astonished to find it served on a spotless dining table among silver and flowers.

The recruiting staff of the WAAF was subjected to bombing in the big cities, and they naturally behaved just as well. At Bristol, the area headquarters and the hotel where the airwomen lived were both hit and three girls killed. Birmingham area headquarters received a direct hit too, and several combined recruiting centres in the south were severely damaged. Despite the Blitz, the London and southeastern area headquarters never failed to send off the daily draft of recruits to the appropriate centre, although the staff and recruits sometimes had to spend half the day in tile shelters, and railway stations were often not functioning.

The Blitz involved many branches of the WAAF, but none more so than the girls on the barrage balloon units. All over the country they won admiration and awards. It was about the time of the Battle of Britain that the Air Council had first explored the chances of replacing valuable RAF manpower on barrage balloon sites with women from its sister service. Training started soon afterwards, and by the time the maximum numbers had been reached, 15,700 WAAF balloon operators were at work, fulfilling the dual function of making low-level enemy air attack impossible, while releasing men.

Life in balloon units was hard and often lonely, with small parties working under the command of a young NCO in areas needing extra protection from air attack. But the girls were happy and became very attached to 'their' balloon, often giving it a name. This might be Baby, Big Bertha, or even, in private, the commanding officer's own nickname!

Apart from the loneliness and toughness of the job, there was also the danger, for the presence of barrage balloons presupposed that here were the very targets the enemy wanted to blast with their nightly cargoes. The WAAF balloon operators knew what might happen to important war factories, docks, marshalling yards or military bases if their particular Baby failed to go up on time. But they soon proved that they could handle the great clumsy creatures in their care. They learned to fill the tough bag with hydrogen, pay out the mooring cable, repair the cables themselves and check the state of the balloon fabric, for a balloon that was not absolutely gas proof would be like a bucket with a hole in it – and about as much use. Before the repairing could be carried out, the girls had to master as many knots, splices and sundry whippings as any able-bodied seaman.

Here are just two of the many cases of gallantry by the girls of the balloon barrage units. Twenty-year-old Corporal Mary was an assistant in a food product distributor in Edinburgh before joining the WAAF. This is her version of an enemy raid on her site:

'Just after the siren had sounded, flares were dropping all round the site and lighting up the sky like day. I sent the crew into the dugout immediately and stayed on the lookout with another airwoman, watching for incendiaries, which I could see were dropping not far away from the site.

'In a little while, two incendiaries dropped on the site just beside the winch, and we put these out quickly with sandbags before they could do any damage. About six others dropped at various parts of the site, some near the hut and on top of the dugout. I called the crew to come and help put them out, but as a matter of fact my call was unnecessary, because they were out asking to help.

'I admit I was a bit nervous, but having found that the first two could be dealt with quite easily, I told the girls how easy it was and they soon became speedy in dealing with other incendiary bombs. One fell through the roof of the wooden hut, and the roof caught fire as well as the table and the floor. We carried out the bomb on a shovel, put it out with sand, and put out all the fires that were blazing in the hut with buckets of water.

'Just outside the site, a Corporation tar boiler was set alight by a further incendiary. We carried this away and put it out, using water and sand to put out the flames on the boiler.'

One warm May night in Wales, Aircraftwoman Lilian Ellis won the British Empire Medal when in charge of No 953 Balloon Barrage, RAF Station, Llandaff. It was 2.31am when the urgent order reached her balloon unit: 'Stand-by.'

Enemy bombers were expected, with their target Cardiff, the source of steel for the war products of Britain.

'Stand by. Stand by.'

The city's balloon barrage was already at 500 feet and within 3 minutes of the alert, the barrage control officer passed the emergency: 'Shine'.

This meant action for the balloon girls. Up strained and soared each balloon to operational height, the heavy cables tautening. Lilian's balloon went up with the rest in the middle of that night.

At 2.41am enemy pathfinders paved the trail of the attack, throbbing and thrusting in first to pinpoint their pre-arranged target with flares that hung over the whole area. Then the bombers brought in the main load. Searchlights stabbed and raked round the sky. Balloons kept the bombers above a low-level altitude. Lilian busily directed her crew to pushing their balloon to the highest point possible. Every aircraft within radius seemed to be hurling high explosives down, and incendiaries started up fires.

On site 53/18, Lilian and her girls watched the raid developing. Bombs came from every height. A kaleidoscope of colour lit the sky. Here and there a plane fell, hit, but the enemy pressed on. It seemed as if Lilian and her crew could not escape.

3.10am, and their bomb came: a direct hit on the site, and with it the squadron's first casualties. Four WAAFs were killed, three others wounded. One of the wounded was Lilian Ellis. But through it all, their balloon kept on flying high, preventing still lower attacks, still worse losses. The ironic thing was that the girls had released RAF personnel for active service, only to find the battle brought home to them as bitterly as it could be: a battle with mortal losses. The girls met the challenge, though, and Lilian's BEM, awarded for her part in keeping their balloon up, could be construed as an honour to all the WAAFs on Balloon Barrage.

But by now the Germans were beginning to get a bit of their own back and the WAAFs were behind these Bomber Command blows. Before the Bomber Command story, however, there comes one WAAF's log to revive those early days more vividly than any official records.

Chapter 3

One WAAF's Log

The first eighteen months of the war were far from all Blitz, however, and WAAFs worked quietly throughout the country on more and more RAF stations. The best way to convey the flavour of those days is to record a WAAF log at a typical station. It happens to be Mount Batten, near Plymouth. The very first arrivals at Mount Batten, way back in October 1939, were three very young teleprinters who came from Wales. They lived out for a week or two in a hostel in Devonport and according to their own account they were as scared of the camp as the camp of them. But soon the original WAAF detachment arrived, nearly two dozen, most of them from the 24th (Devon) Company. To a large extent, they were already known to each other, for they were just a little section of the unwieldy mass who assembled on Fridays from all parts of Devon and Cornwall at Beaumont House in Plymouth.

'The original detachment were much thrilled by the little houses – late married quarters – into which they were shown, but failed to sleep with any success for several nights and without exception acquired the most deplorable colds, Mount Batten being rather bleak and blowy in late October for the uninitiated and the bed "biscuits" hard on first acquaintance. In addition, the houses had been empty for several weeks and both walls and sheets were very damp.

'There were two little dining rooms, two sitting room cookers and two cooks. It was all most exciting and everyone was tremendously keen and very frightened, too shy to walk down the camp unaccompanied and not dreaming to be so bold as to speak to an airman. It always appears strange to the originals that latter recruits, with a WAAF detachment firmly at their backs, did not have that overwhelming awe of the Air Force. Nor did they, for that matter, have the Air Force prejudice to conquer.

'WAAF recruits of today are accepted as a matter of course, but in those days Mount Batten was just like all other Air Force camps in the early war days – outwardly quite polite, but inwardly a good deal resentful. There was an equipment assistant amongst these "more than rookies" who was posted to the then squadron attached – 204 – and before her arrival their CO warned all in the cubbyhole where she was to work that they must be extremely careful not to swear in her presence. The men carried out his order so literally that the WAAF was driven to think that there was something extremely odd about them, though she could not make out what. One day she made a more than usually drastic mistake and swore loudly, at which they all hooted and decided to be natural. Six months later, they were posted to a war station, and she, the only WAAF in their squadron, almost broke her heart at their being left behind.

'For the majority it took some time to get accepted. No one could quite put a finger on the moment, fasten it and say, "This was when they altered to us." A particular dance was remembered, though, the first one the WAAF gave just before Christmas 1939. The gym was gaily decorated; no effort had been grudged so that this, their first function, could be a success. The WAAFs attired themselves in their prettiest evening frocks – there were no uniforms then – and the start of surprise when the first arrivals appeared and beheld some decent-looking girls will always be remembered by those particular WAAFs.

'The WAAF did look rather like unclaimed bundles that winter everywhere. The chief benefit of the raincoats was that one could wear infinite layers of clothes underneath and still "go up round the belt", but the resulting shape was not exactly sylph-like.

Without expatiating on a winter that all experienced alike, let it only be said that Mount Batten was like a typhoon–swept desert island on the extreme tip of the North Pole. If one ventured across in the ferry to Plymouth, it was a case of trusting in God and the nearest outstretched hand as one made one's way down the slippery steps of the breakwater in the blackout. If the tide were low, there was a terrific leap downwards; if full, the sea was definitely rough. Certainly it was only God who knew whether the ferry would run back again – Arthur the ferryman disclaimed all responsibility.

'We slept in the icy-cold bedrooms without thought of complaint, but we had one sitting room to every two houses, eight to a sitting room; it was very homely, except of course that there was a lot of smoke and the bath water varied from pale brown to deep rust red. There was squash, fencing, and table tennis. A room inspection once a week, on Mondays. No one dreamed of "stacking" beds, and it is safe to say that they only got a straighten very seldom. Brooms were not terrifically in demand, except on a Sunday evening – a sublimely beautiful state of affairs, which could not be expected to last indefinitely.

'Plymouth rain is famous all the world over. Mount Batten rain, egged on by all the winds that blow across her narrow neck of land, is guaranteed to reduce WAAF berets to the size of boot buttons and to get well down anyone's coat collar. On morning parade, standing on the ice-coated ground, with Batten's particular brand of sleet finding its way into all the unprotected nooks and crannies of one's person, it was sometimes difficult to say one's prayers with proper devotion.

'At first the tiny squad was inclined to giggle as it was marched right through the camp. It seemed that only a few picks and shovels were needed to give credence to the sensation that it was a convict squad, but in a remarkably short space of time, the parade was accepted as part of the ritual of this still-novel life. Nothing, in fact, could daunt the enthusiasm of those early WAAFs who were inwardly so convinced that they were each just one more nail in Hitler's coffin.

'That conviction was doomed to slip a trifle. Perhaps it was contact with the regulars, perhaps the glorious Batten summer. We had joined up to help win the war, but we found ourselves provided with our own lido and bathing place, our own tennis court. We went for walks to Down Thomas and picnics to Jennysands and other glorious bathing spots.

'We could easily put up with having to rise at 6.30 instead of 7.30 in order to stack our beds and do our cleaning, though at first it seemed a monstrous idea: indeed, we were so indignant that when at first asked by our new officer if we knew how to stack beds, we all nodded our heads wisely, refusing to admit ignorance. Everyone trusted that someone else would know this great military secret. Some said, "You stagger the bed and make it into an armchair, one biscuit at the back and one each side." Some actually attempted to do this, so that the sergeant admin had a most strenuous time next morning rushing from room to room and exclaiming despairingly: "But why didn't you say you didn't know and we could have had a demonstration!"

'We could put up with regular drills and even PT at a pinch the only drawback was that we were consistently much too hot. New WAAFs had come so steadily that our detachment had swelled to more than double its original number. We accepted the new rules and regulations. Plunged into a glorious summer, the general idea seemed to be to have a good time in spite of them – very different from the rather naïve idea of the original WAAFs.

'Then, quite suddenly, the bottom fell out of the glorious blue sky. The refugees came, hundreds of them, and at first sight mostly black. It was a Sunday and we had come up from the camp at midday to our quarters for dinner when lorry load after lorry load turned in at the gate. We stood outside our houses and waved to them and they, in spite of their tiredness and hunger and the grim experiences so recently endured, grinned back and gave the English thumbs-up. There were French, Belgians and Moroccans, literally starving. For three weeks they had not had a proper meal; for ten days they had been on the run. The Moroccans had been torpedoed three times on the way over; three times they had been nearly drowned and only a proportion rescued. They scared us a bit. The Europeans would not mix with them, and they lay out in the broiling sun on the football field, immobile and utterly unsmiling. They all had trench feet and several were injured, but wild horses would not drive them to the medical officer. The French and Belgians were very different; polite, excessively grateful, and eager to speak with anyone who could converse with them. What they did say was soon all over the camp, as if they had spoken to each individual. "The guns, the tanks, masses of them. Human beings couldn't stand out against them. And the aeroplanes – where were ours?"

'That was the first night. It was different next morning when they had all had a good rest, a wash, and time to clean their kit. It impressed us how so many of them had managed to hang on to their heavy kit. They looked disciplined, undaunted and gravely determined to get away and back again to the fight. They disappeared as suddenly as they had come, but not before they had spared thanks for the food, for the men who had stood to serve their own dinners to the refugees, and for the cooks and washers-up who had worked like galley slaves.

'It was strange to see the football field quite empty again, not littered with those prone forms. We had had a shock. Like an icy-cold shower, startling. We felt that the front line had got very near to us; that we might, in fact, be the front line before very long.

'We were fully in training for our next batch of visitors – the Air Force survivors of the *Lancastria*, the British Cunard liner that was sunk on 17 June 1940 and in which around 4,000 people died. There was a phone call late at night for our officer, our sergeant admin and our medical orderly to go down and help, as these men were being rushed straight to the camp. Some were sent straight off in ambulances and other came ashore at Mount Batten at midnight. They were bedded down in the gym, all in a state of extreme exhaustion and clad for the most part in wristwatches and identity discs, a blanket, or half a naval boiler suit.

'The majority of men were unhurt physically, but very sick from the oil they had swallowed. They had cuts and scratches and were all filthy from the oil, and many of them were too weak to wash themselves. The ration store was raided for tinned fruit, which some ate thankfully before they sank into heavy sleep. The RAF and WAAF who were permitted the opportunity laboured for them into the morning and the camp woke up to find another band of visitors with whom to share their meals and their cigarettes.

'Roll call was held – a sad business, for the toll had been heavy. All day one saw these men scanning every other man's face hopefully and wistfully. Twice a lorry load arrived and the scene was most un-British. At Devonport, they had separated the Forces, but some had gone the wrong way and now their comrades crowded round as each new arrival, given up for lost, was hauled down, hugged and cheered.

'That night, after the men's first day of readjusting themselves to being alive, our WAAF officer had a whip-round for all available WAAFs who had not left camp to go down to the gym in their coolest civvies, because it was very hot and the gym very crowded. That was our night. There was no room for more men, and it was us they wanted. Not WAAFs, but girls with whom they could dance, to prove that everything was normal again. They unburdened themselves on to us and we felt that we served a useful function in encountering them to get the worst of it off their chests before they went home on leave. Afterwards, one of them said to our officer that it was the WAAFs who had saved their sanity.

'Certainly it had been a horrible experience for them – to wait all those long hours on the ship for the convoy, which was too late, packed like sardines, tens of hundreds with distressed women and children. Then as their convoy at last hove into sight, the dive-bombing started, the first bomb dropping sheer through the funnel into the engine room. It was then that all the oil was released, in an effort to save the ship from fire. All those who had managed to swarm on the decks were ordered to one side to try and right her – and it was from this height that they had to jump, into a thick surface of oil many feet deep.

'We listened to tales of heroism and tragedy, but it was remarkable how soon they pulled themselves together. The atmosphere changed, as if now they had put it all behind them. There were one or two who sat apart, slightly injured, on the few beds, others footsore or still rather ill who reclined on the blankets, and others writing letters home happily in all the din.

'It must have been about this time that the seven-day-week, no-half-day, no-leave-for-everyone period started, and the airmen took to carrying rifles, which they only hoped they would be able to use. The engineer officer, on being asked by his MT sergeant what he was to do with his WAAF drivers should the camp be invaded, said "Do with them? What can we do? If the Boches come, it'll be each man for himself, and Christ help us all."

'The sergeant said, a little daunted, "Seems to me, sir, that in their billets, they'll be in the front line." The officer did not ask the sergeant how he knew that the Boches would walk in at the main gate!

'One memorable evening we thought that the invasion had actually started. All the WAAFs were confined to their billets, and from the windows we watched the men, RAF and Australians, file up the road with the strange and fearsome-looking rifles on their shoulders. Some threw jokes at us, treating it all in a grand spirit of bravado, but most of them looked rather white. To us, as they filed up Staddon, it did not look a very goodly number. Our newly converted Crossley, the "armoured car" with its one little gun, brought up the rear. We just sat tight and felt unusually hungry, and presently they all came back. Next day, of course, they declared that they had guessed it was just a practice.

'Another morning, shortly after this, we were roused by the bugle, which at that time meant for the men "Grab your rifle and run to your appointed post." Most of the WAAFs dressed hastily, thinking that they would rather be captured clothed than otherwise. As it turned out, these careful WAAFs reaped the benefit because there was an early morning air raid. There were quite a number of alarms then, round about 7am, which was awkward as the WAAF officer then had an excellent opportunity of judging, by the state of general dressed-ness, whether the official time of getting up had been complied with or not. All kinds of ingenious excuses were forthcoming of course: "I was scrubbing out the bathroom in my birthday suit, Ma'am" ... and so on, and so on.

'No one dreamed then of not obeying the siren. We had no dugouts or shelters for the billets, but we used to hare across the fields to the new ops room, in course of construction. It was in the days when the enemy was occasionally daring, and one Sunday at 5pm he had suddenly dived down out of the clouds without warning and machine-gunned us. Did we come out of our houses and take to our heels! It gave us quite a pleasant thrill – as did our first small guns. We did not dream that six months later we should boast the most deafening barrages in the country and, oblivious of orders, continue to sit on in our rooms more often than not – unless the bombs had started falling – merely raising our voice to be heard above the din.

'It was at this time, when the news was so bad and there were no half days, that some of the WAAFs, having dutifully put their front flower gardens in order, started enthusiastically on the backs. The deeper one dug in the gardens at Batten, the more impossible it got. The builders seemed to have discarded more cement and bricks and general rubble than they put into the houses themselves. It was backbreaking work, entirely beyond any tool but a pickaxe. The soldiers opposite, however, a very nice batch of 10th Devons, had a gun emplacement overlooking the back gardens, and a technique was gradually developed by the WAAFs by which the lookers-on changed places with the workers, to the encouragement of much tactfully expressed awe of superior male muscle, rewarded by sundry cups of tea and small services with needle and thread. We planted cabbages and broccoli, lettuce and cauliflower, and to our delight they came to fruition without any treatment but with lots of surreptitious watering.

'The Australian squadron, who came after our beloved 204 left us in March, were not such a menace to our morale as was first expected. It was rumoured before the Aussies came that the WAAFs might all be posted, as it was not policy to have WAAFs in the same camp as overseas men. After this, our expectation was at fever pitch and we fully expected to have to cling firmly and desperately to our hearts. The result was disappointing. On the whole, they did not fire either our imaginations or our hearts, and no out-and-out romance came to pass. In fact, there were only two inter-camp marriages to report: a WAAF medical orderly to an RAF corporal ditto, and a WAAF to an RAF 204 warrant officer.

'The first wedding – when one of our first WAAF corporals married a civilian – was a picturesque ceremony in the village church of Brixton, which a batch of the original WAAF attended. As the squadron leader (equipment) pointed out in his speech, it was scarcely a hasty wartime affair, as the pair had known each other for over five years! Corporal Rogers was a storybook bride, tall, dark, and interestingly pale, beautifully garbed in white satin. The bridesmaids wore deep yellow, matching the village hall, which was hung with frilly curtains of yellow crinkled paper by a fellow WAAF. The village children gazed wide-eyed at us as we managed to clink into our lorry after having several times been offered the choice of "tea or sherry". After a visit to the bride's parents' house to view the presents, we came back to camp again singing lustily.

'We had our steel helmets then, so the wedding must have been subsequent to our first daylight air raid of any importance. For two months or so, we had been having two or three raids per night, dutifully arousing ourselves each time, grabbing our blankets and trekking for our new shelters. We would just get off to sleep when the all-clear would go, and back we would go to bed – and just get off to sleep once more when off the siren would go again.

'It was summer, so perhaps it was easier to take it then. The only days when we overslept were the rare occasions when we had had a full night's rest. We were well on our way to our hundredth raid before the blitz on London started.

'It was news, writing home, to say that we'd had no raid, otherwise it was just stale. In any case, they were not at all exciting. At first we felt moved to sing to show we were brave (about what we can't now imagine). Later we were just bored – and sometimes cross, on the third rousing in one night when there wasn't room for everyone to lie down in the shelter.

'Two nights were exceptions, when we heard the men on the guns cheer when a Dornier was brought down, and again when four were destroyed. There was one ship in which we all put our faith. When the *Cromarty* went out of the Cattewater, we all felt we had lost our bodyguard, and as soon she was sighted again, it went round the camp in no time: "It's all right, the *Cromarty*'s back." Her master was always first off the mark with his gun, but Jerry soon learnt just how high and no higher the *Cromarty* could fire.

'Our daylight raid, however, was the most exciting we had yet experienced. On the sound of the siren, we came out of our offices to see a plane overhead, which we imagined must surely be a Spitfire. It swooped low before our gaze and dropped a stick of bombs plum into the centre of the camp. We dived, scrambled, or were blown into the dugouts, then after a few more ominous sounds we were somewhat taken aback to hear the all clear. We trooped out again, only to see the same Jerry make a second swoop with a second stick of bombs descending on us.

'When we discovered that there were no casualties, we were exhilarated by the experience, but we had a few very nasty moments until we were assured that the sergeants' mess WAAFs had managed to get out in time. A bomb dropped on the sergeants' billiards table and they missed it dreadfully. The old ops room, vacated for the new one only twelve hours previously, was destroyed, and among other places the new airmen's institute, barely completed, was badly hit.

'It was the afternoon before we were to move into WAAFville, our new mess. A hundred pounds had been spent on the disused golf pavilion, now in the confines of the camp, on a new cooking stove, other domestic improvements and generally poshing it up. The chart was made out, listing which bits each of us were to spring clean, and after that we were to have linoleum laid and new furniture fitted, tables and chairs for the mess room, and rugs and cane chairs for the lounge. Our number now varying from fifty to sixty, we had long outgrown our two little dining rooms in the married quarters.

'We were doomed, however, not to move into WAAFville till early November: their mess being so much more bombed about, the sergeants took possession. WAAF M and K staff, bombed out at 3pm, moved into WAAFville with what remained of their gear and had a cooked tea ready at 6.30pm. Even the sergeants were moved to express gratification!

'Everyone was highly amused that Jerry should have picked on the sergeants, and sure enough he did it again, but to a lesser extent, on 27 November. By that time, we had got careless about raids, our excuse being that in the midst of all the guns it was impossible to hear the new little klaxon on the Mount, which exhorted all and sundry that now was the time to come out and dodge the shrapnel.

When suddenly issued with latex ear-cones, we were gratified but slightly amused – though secretly we knew that one day we would get it from Jerry, and we did.

'On Wednesday 27 November, the sirens went off at about 6.30pm, unnoticed as usual. Then a gun or two; then close on the heels of this the most terrific thuds, which brought everyone to their doors to see several fires in all directions and without a doubt one of them was our hangar. Ten Squadron's, to be precise. We scurried to the shelters with helmets and the ever-useful cushion of a respirator, but without our erstwhile amenities of blankets and other aids to comfort. We sat there till 2.40am, having made up our minds that we should none of us come out of the shelter alive. Between whistles of bombs, which we were not to know were falling with monotonous regularity up in the fields at Staddon, we managed to laugh and joke, with slightly unnatural vim at times, and the hours passed to the extent of two new candles burnt consecutively. We were glad that nothing more should be demanded of us at the moment but that we should sit still and pretend we were not at all alarmed. A/S/O Fuller nobly ventured out for an armful of blankets, but came back with some beautiful white Sick Bay ones well muddied and her spectacles lost. Our section officer seemed to have a grand time, throwing herself prone between visits to shelters and gathering news.

'We got appallingly hungry, of course, but all we were offered on emerging was a drink of beer, so we took ourselves to bed, where we slept like tops – except for some who had to be on duty in the airmen's mess at five, and who doubtless spent what remained of their leisure in wondering how many bomb craters they would fall into in the dark or their way to work.

'What was so trying about that blitz of ours, though, was not the damage done, though we lost two of our precious boats, and there was also quite a lot of damage on the camp, but the fire. It was an extra-large-size one in Turnchapel village, not ten minutes' walk away. By day the smoke rolled mightily into the sky, no flames at all. But as soon as darkness fell, all that smoke was pure flame, not a weenie drift of smoke. There were five oil tanks and two of petrol. Floodlighting was nothing to it. You could read a newspaper in the

Plymouth street across the Cattewater, and during those four long days and three nights, the guards at the main gate outside our doors ceased to yell if a tiny chink of light was accidentally to show. We have only to open the front doors of our billets and a great gust of heat would blow in.

'The experts said that there was devil-or-nothing anyone could do about the fire. It just had to burn at its own speed, one inch per hour, and on Thursday morning we were told it would be out by 7pm on the Sunday. The whole of Turnchapel and most of Hooe were evacuated. There had been casualties in the villages, but miraculously, again, no one actually in the camp had been killed.

'Naturally we expected not one more blitz but three, for when again would Jerry have such a superb opportunity of wiping out Plymouth, and, incidentally, our camps? But no, he was yellow. He came each night, and dropped encouragement on the fire, which needed none, and on the villages round about, and reported to his master that "Plymouth was in flames."

'With all the civilians gone and our boats evacuated, we livened things up as best we could, and would be informed each day at tea that "as this was probably our last meal" we could have whatever we wanted – within reason. No eggs today, though.

'The next thrill subsequent to our blitz-which-didn't-come was the arrival of our greatcoats. It was almost, but not quite, as great a thrill to the originals as the long-awaited arrival of our uniforms, and then there was a worry about fittings. The greatcoats, marvellously, fitted. We had been promised them, but only vaguely; we feared it would be March or possibly April before they got as far south as us. Then, without warning, fifty arrived, but they were for our outstations: outstations supposedly more bleak than us, though we know of one which is a Palace of Luxury inside, whatever it may be like without. Hot and cold water in your bedroom, if you please, and armchairs, which assuredly never figured in any Air Force vocabulary. Eight outstations meant a good many more than fifty greatcoats, but on 7 December, to be exact, we were told to report to Equipment at 2pm precisely. Were we pleased with them? They felt good and looked good and were beyond our wildest expectations.

Very, very different from the "concerted men's", which was the lot of the luckier WAAFs last winter, and which, topped with a rain-shrunken beret, and did not compete successfully with the resplendent Auxiliary Territorial Service (ATS).

'The men were almost as admiring of us as we were! "Ten buttons to clean," they gloated, but enviously. "But of course," said a senior NCO, "no one dreams of cleaning their inner buttons in the winter time!" As a matter of fact, we wouldn't be without one single, glittering button, and we certainly would not have been in the ATS or the WRNS for the entire world. Khaki only suits a very few and the poor Wrens had to wear black stockings.

'Just to keep us in the fashion, Jerry decided to treat us to another fire-blitz. Before the sirens had stopped their mournful wail, Plymouth was well alight, and as HEs were also to the fore, the shelter seemed a good idea. The fireworks were certainly well worth watching, and the shrapnel pitter-pattered down on the houses like sleet. The same thing was going on all over the camp: over 150 incendiaries were counted, but there were probably a good deal more. The Group Captain's house was honoured; the workshops had six; and every building a proportionate number. Needless to say, the sergeants' mess was again slightly damaged by an HE, and at one moment the ops room was a quaint sight with the flame leaping over it, the camouflage creeper having caught. Every single fire was put out in its earliest stages.

'So Christmas came. We had a delightful week, with late passes every night and no morning parades. On Christmas Day, we had our dinner at 5.30pm: roast turkey, roast pork, plum pudding, mince pies and beer to drink. The WAAF officers waited and the gas officer did the carving. In the evening, we were invited down to the sergeants' mess, which was so successful that it is proposed to make it a monthly affair.

'The camp pantomime was *Sunderella*, a poor little airman who, given fatigues in the officers' mess, acquired from the fairy godmother two lots of wings for a twin-engine bomber. But it all ended, of course, at 11.59pm, when he had to book in.

Chapter 4

Bomber Command

After the Battle of Britain, Bomber Command began to come into its own. Aircraft were being built and crews trained, and it was a Wellington bomber on a training flight that became the means of Corporal Alice Holden proving herself.

With her hair the regulation distance from her blue collar, Alice got ready to go on duty a hundred times as radio-telephonist. Her voice over the R/T and those of many WAAFs like her spelled the safety of home for bomber crews talked down to land at all the air stations such as Wittering. It had been here at Wittering that a commanding officer had ordered all WAAFs away from the airfield when enemy raiders were known to be approaching in 1940. They had obeyed the order, of course, but protested so strongly that the CO never gave the order again.

Since those days, airmen had come and gone through Alice's watches in Flying Control there, with new voices always ready to replace those that fell silent. Sometimes the radio homing channel jammed with calls to Control for radio help in getting back to base. Plane after plane would bound triumphantly along the tarmac, lightening the long watch. But somehow it was those missing voices the WAAFs remembered most. Time and again, Alice's thoughts were projected to a certain scene as the plane she was talking to over the air struggled to get out of difficulties. Often they failed. And there was nothing Alice could do about it.

But stand-by duty was perhaps the worst of all, she thought, as she sipped a cup of tea during her ten o'clock break on the night of 24 October 1943. It was frustrating to have virtually nothing to do when so much was happening all around. By now Alice had left Wittering and was on a Lincolnshire air station. Once she had finished her tea, she felt too restless for the rest room, so wandered out into the crisp night air of autumn. While she walked about aimlessly outside the control room, a Wellington bomber – or Wimpey, as it was affectionately known – on a routine training flight was approaching this south-west corner of the county. Soon Alice would be doing much more than stand-by duty.

As the pilot let down through the cloud to check his position, the plane went out of control long enough to fall into a steep dive. Alice held her breath and then, by the very sound of it, knew the moment when the pilot regained control. The Wimpey was leveling off – too late. The inexperienced crew were encountering that formidable factor 'g' the force of gravity, and losing the fight. Lower, lower, the Wimpey came, then crashed, grounding grotesquely some 150 yards from the control room. The noise of the crash reached Alice in an instant, as her eyes were riveted on the wreckage. Flames attacked the fuselage. She reacted at once. She sprinted into the race with fire, as if she had been training for this moment all her life.

As she neared the plane, its exploding petrol tanks rocked her backwards. The Wimpey hurled a barrage of metal fragments at her. Alice registered several near misses and ran on regardless. By then, flames virtually enveloped the sixty-foot-long latticed fuselage. She heard cries for help, but could not distinguish their origins. Drowned by the shifting roar of burning, they seemed to switch position. How many of the crew of five still survived?

As Alice edged towards the rear turret of the disintegrating bomber, the cries resolved into the voice of one man – the rear gunner, alive in his turret. The turret looked like a blazing cage, fastened to the tail end of the plane, and through its transparent walls the glare of the fire burnished the form of Sergeant Buckley. Whether on ops over enemy territory or as here, in a crash, Tail-End Charlie was a man apart. And his isolation from the rest of the crew now served him well. With the whole length of the fuselage to absorb the shock of impact, the rear gunner had the best chance to survive. He was alive, yes, but trapped in his turret. The same perspex that protected a rear gunner from attacking fighters was also unbreakable from within the turret. Alice saw that Buckley did not even try.

The turret had swung round on its revolving mechanism to a sideways position, but the steel escape doors refused to slide open. The seconds took on a quality outside time as flames tore at the turret. The gunner's fingers clutched instinctively at the surrounding steel. The very transparency of the cage made his fate more ironic. Buckley had given up calling his comrades over the intercom. They had been his only company through the hours of that flight. Now there was no answer. He was alone with the flames. The turret grew stifling.

He shouted for help at the depth of his lungs. The reverberation within the confined space was earsplitting. But could his voice pass through the perspex and rise above the roar of the fire? He knew that a fire-tender might already be on its way, but as his senses and his eyes blurred, he knew it might come too late. Time ticked.

He had learned how to cope with a Focke-Wulfe at twelve o'clock high. He would swing his guns into position, call out manoeuvring instructions to the pilot, and fire away. It was the enemy or you. To die in the heat of battle, with your crew depending on you and an enemy to face – that was one thing. But this heat was something else. Grounded and trapped in your own Wimpey.

He shook his head sharply. He closed his eyes and shouted again and again. He opened his eyes, frowning as he peered through the enflamed perspex. Then it was that he saw Alice. He had never been so glad to see anyone in his life. He waved wildly. 'Go for help,' he mouthed. 'Steel escape doors stuck. Need men enough to force them. Hurry.'

The intensity of the heat as well as the words drove Alice away from the plane, but the reaction was only momentary. There was no time to go for help. She knew that. Instead she forced herself towards the turret. The panels of steel – they were the goal. She reached them, and the two of them tugged away at these doors, he from inside and she from outside. To Buckley the plane was like an oven; to Alice, a furnace. Between them they pulled with every muscle they could muster.

The doors slid open. Buckley hurled himself backwards into the open air as flames scorched inside, as if in search of the ammunition stored along the sides of his seat. Alice leapt aside to make way for his fall to earth, but it was not to be. His parachute webbing got entangled somehow and thwarted his somersault out of that hell. Cramped in his position, encumbered by the heavy white sweater under his Irvin jacket, hazy from the heat, tormented by the flames, Buckley could not free himself from the perverse webbing. Alice desperately yanked on the harness. It was actually smouldering and the blaze nibbled at Buckley's clothes. He was waiting for the bullets in the ammunition belts. They must come any moment now. If Alice had not been trying to help him, he would have thought this was a nightmare. He tottered towards unconsciousness and with a despairing gesture tried to wave Alice away. 'Save yourself,' he would have said if he could.

But he reckoned without this girl. Together they somehow struggled with his harness again. The life-saving parachute looked as if it might cost him his. The frantic tug-of-war went on and seemed endless until a final wrench freed him. He could not really believe it – he had given himself up several minutes earlier.

Safety still lay a few yards off, so Alice quickly grasped him under the armpits and hauled him clear. They emerged through an orange curtain of fire. From the outside, it appeared impossible for anyone to have lived and walked through it. Then it was an ambulance and a hospital bed for Sergeant Buckley and a gong for Alice. She received the British Empire Medal the following year for 'courage and devotion to duty'. One might almost say beyond the call of duty, as she was only on 'stand-by' at the time!

Exhilarating as this exploit was, the day-to-day duties of Bomber Command WAAFs were more typical and equally vital to the overall RAF effort. Their work was like that of WAAF Sergeant Audrey Smith, who gives the following accurate account of her life as a Clerk/Special Duties (Watchkeeper) Bomber Command.

'This trade was entered after taking a test in front of Board of Bomber Command personnel. Officers and a psychiatrist were present. Requirements: general commonsense, good general knowledge, a cool head in an emergency, integrity, devotion to detail and a good telephone voice.

'One began as an under-training watchkeeper, usually with rank of LACW gaining two stripes and then three rather more quickly than in other trades because of the attendant responsibility.

'Usually there were three sergeants on each station working three watches: 1pm to 8 pm the first day; 8am to 1pm the following morning and afternoon off, resuming watching at 8 in the evening until 8 the following morning. This varied according to station; sometimes a four-watch system was worked.

'You worked alone in the ops room, naturally under the jurisdiction of the intelligence officers who were nearby and, of course, were visited during the course of the day by station CO, flight commanders, bombing, engineering and met officers and so on.

'The whole day was spent receiving broadcasts, taken over scrambler phones from Command via Group; these were taken down on three-ply teleprinter paper, with inserted carbon clipped to a board. Copies of these were given to CO and relevant personnel. But everything, repeat *everything*, was logged in a big book. This was your bible. You put time of receipt of message, contents of same, to whom given and time given. This was most important. Anything that went wrong could be checked back to this book and woe betide the watchkeeper who forgot to enter some detail while she was boiling a kettle or was up the large double-sided ladder provided for her to reach the large blackboard at one end of the ops room, giving details of each squadron, such as aircraft letters, captain and crews' names, bomb loads, estimated times of departure, over targets, and return times. The whole day was spent in the receipt and dissemination of all details concerning a bombing raid.

'Once target and loads, aircraft requirements and so on were received, the ball started rolling. There were flight-planning conferences held. This was carried out in the presence of the CO, the squadron commanders and so on sitting in the ops room listening to Group through a loudspeaker and being able to have interchanges of conversations with Group and the other stations in the Group through pressing various switches on the small board affixed to the watchkeeper's desk.

'As the day wore on, there were briefing times to be worked out, winds and cloud bases for the met officers to calculate, meal times to be arranged with the messing officer, and flying meals for return of aircraft from raid.

'Once squadron passed the flying schedule, this was passed through to Group and chalked on blackboard. Signals were received from nearby teleprinter rooms. Positions of convoys were received at periodic intervals. These were plotted with chinagraph pencil on the mica surface of the plotting table, usually located in middle of ops room floor.

'In the event of non-operational flying, clearance had to be obtained from the local Fighter Group. Certain lanes of exit over the coast had to be adhered to and SD158 was our second bible, giving details of balloon centres, ack-ack and searchlight emplacements. Also a jettison area was available in North Sea for aircraft that had to make early returns due to engine failures and like reasons, having to eject their bomb load into sea.

'Despite necessary formal atmosphere, there was a great deal of informality, such as unending cups of tea being made and drunk by all and sundry. Night rations were provided in the shape of tea, sugar, tinned milk, eggs, bacon, bread, and sometimes a pork chop!

'Contact was maintained all the time with Flying Control, who rang through as each aircraft took off, or returned – the relevant details being passed to Group. On return of aircraft, each crew went to Intelligence Section where they were interrogated by RAF and WAAF officers, the latter also keeping records of crew flying hours, and others involved in such duties as photographic interpretation.

'One night there may be no operational flying and one settled down in the bed provided to have a nap between possible phone calls and signals. Then sometimes there would be a quick broadcast from Group and a surprise operation put on – it was out of bed quickly and into action.

'One day the morning broadcast announced "There will be a Command stand-down tonight – no flying – make and mend." This latter phrase meant attention to servicing aircraft and making good repairs. That same night, around 2100 hours, local Fighter Group kept ringing and saying "British aircraft have just crossed coast at Cromer heading out to sea," to which one could only reply, "I only know that there is a Command stand–down tonight." For hours we kept querying aircraft movements. Then about four the following morning, intelligence clerk burst into operations room saying: "Guy Gibson's just breached the Moehne dam, great parts of Germany are flooded!" This was surely one of the best-kept secrets of the war.

'One amusing night was spent in an ops room of a station on the Great North Road; a small ops room, not underground, with windows all round, situated beneath the F/Control tower. A message from War Office Intelligence at about 2300 hours was to the effect that there was a suspicion of an attempted mass breakout of German prisoners. This really frightened me and I went round religiously barring all doors – naturally after informing the necessary people on the station. But in the morning I found two windows open. If the Germans had arrived they would have had easy access to the operations block!

'Also on duty that night with me was Nemo, the F/Control cat, who was a source of company. Imagine the Flying Control officer's amazement on passing a window and hearing me saying, 'Well, Nemo, it's only you and me against the Germans, we mustn't let the station down.' The cat merely asked in his own fashion for a little more of the milk ration. The Germans didn't come after all, but a doodlebug arrived sometime during the dawn, landing in the vicinity of Newark/Trent.

'On another occasion a complaint was received by telephone from the mayor of Scarborough that aircraft were practice-bombing the town. These were Australian personnel being just a little too daring. A report to Station CO and official apologies were made.

'Sometimes visibility clamped down and if base was unfit for return, some or indeed all aircraft had to be diverted to a station in south of England, very often Manston. Aircraft returning from raid that did not show up after some two hours' interval and checking of other stations were regarded as missing and one had to pass through names of crew to Air Ministry AS4 Holborn for relay to next of kin. One night an aircraft was lost with all the senior officers on board: squadron commander, navigating officer, flight engineering officer, gunnery officer, signals officer. We had the unenviable task of ringing the wing commander's wife the next morning and giving her the sad news, always stressing that aircraft may have landed somewhere and we had not yet been told. So crews had amazing adventures: one in particular came down inside Allied lines in Belgium and walked home! There were watchkeepers, of course, who were possibly engaged to missing crews. It was very hard for these girls.

'It was a most stimulating job being a watchkeeper and because of shift work and sleeping hours and time off one was able to evade quite a lot of admin duties – I hope this doesn't sound too naughty!

'However, there was a colour hoisting parade each morning outside of one ops block in which I worked. So many aircrew were detailed, so many WAAF of which I would be in charge, and an officer would take the parade. This was very thinly attended at times, aircrew finding various excuses for not being there.

'There was a tremendous thrill and pride to the job and regret (though one hardly regrets the coming of peace, naturally) when there were no longer lines of aircraft taking off into the dusk; large black Lancasters, their navigation lights winking green and red like coloured stars. There was a tremendous camaraderie between WAAF sergeant and the officers she worked with, and a sense of being treated as an equal, at the same time, of course, knowing one's place! This could not be repeated when one returned to civilian life.

That was the WAAF as Sergeant Audrey Smith saw it. While she kept watch, airwomen were helping the Bomber Command offensive in many other ways. For instance, aircrews of squadrons taking part in this mounting attack depended for the efficient running of their aircraft on the accumulator batteries, which were tested and maintained by WAAFs in electrical workshops.

This was a responsible job, for not only the success of the raid, but the lives of the crews hinged on the skill and care put into the servicing of the batteries. If this failed, the switch panel, crowded with its complex instruments and gauges, went out of action. Without it a night bomber pilot could not carry on. More than this, it would also put out of order the rear gunner's turret and his guns that defended the bomber against surprise fighter attack from that direction. The accumulators fed all the most essential controls of the aircraft, including the bomb door and the bomb release switch.

In a hut on the edge of an airfield of Bomber Command, an eighteen-year-old airwoman – a shop assistant before the war – was busy servicing her batteries for Lancasters. The walls of her workshop were lined with black and chromium charging boards, while on wooden trestles below were ranged anything up to thirty-six accumulators waiting to be topped up and tested. WAAF charging board operators were given an intensive course on this work and were fully alive to the vital nature of the task.

'It takes two days to charge a battery,' the aircraftwoman said as she fitted the charging board leads to a set of batteries from an aircraft that had taken part in a raid on Essen. 'When I finished my course, I charged batteries for the flashing beacon and flare paths. That was exciting, but this job is much more responsible, and I like to think that my batteries went all the way to Essen and back.'

In a dozen different ways, the WAAFs were behind the bomber crews, and amenities improved all the time as the offensive went on and the strain on aircrew grew.

The crew of a Halifax squadron returning from a raid on Berlin went straight from their aircraft to a new drying room opened for them on their station under the care of a WAAF safety equipment assistant. This was the latest 1943 method of taking perfect care of flying kit and safety equipment used on operations. LACW 'Margaret', a WAAF veteran of two years' service, was one of the first airwomen in Bomber Command to undertake this job. She worked in a long, concrete-floored hut heated to a regular temperature by special pipes. At one end of the hut ran shelves lined with ready-packed parachutes and safety gear, and at the other end rows of wooden peg-stands for flying kit. Each crew had its own stand, and the floor beneath the pegs was neatly squared off with the words 'Navigator', 'Pilot' or 'Air gunner' so that the bulky kit could not get mixed. Each man's helmet, boots and fur-lined jacket could be instantly identifiable and made available.

Briefing over for the next trip, the crews swarmed into the drying room to collect their gear before the operational tea. Margaret knew them all and scarcely needed to check: 'Navigator of T for Tommy?' before going to T for Tommy's stand and taking down a helmet and a Mae West from the navigator's personal peg.

'Good luck.'

'Thanks. See you in the morning.'

Whistling quietly to himself, the navigator went off. By the time she saw him next, he would have been to Berlin and back. Sometimes it seemed unreal to Margaret.

The engines crackled into life, the planes nosed along the runway, and all was suddenly very quiet. Some would not return. Perhaps T for Tommy. Once the take-off was over, Margaret snatched a few hours' sleep, until the welcome sound of the first bomber back droning overhead warned her that in five or ten minutes the crews would be coming in to return their gear. She never minded turning out of bed, for this was the most thrilling part to her: to know that she would be one of the first to talk to the airmen after their return from the raid. And seeing them straggling in, tired but still cheerful, Margaret felt glad that she was responsible for maintaining all their equipment that kept them warm and protected them in an emergency on an op such as this.

T for Tommy got back safely. The navigator smiled at her as he dumped his gear. He would not need it for a while: until the next time. Life revolved around ops – could be measured by them, often.

By 1943, WAAF intelligence officers were helping in the tiring but necessary task of interrogating bomber crews from most of the large-scale raids such as this one on Berlin. Once their gear had been safely stowed, the aircrews trooped over to the ops block where the intelligence officers were waiting to hear their stories. The men were worn out after eight hours' night flying, much of it over enemy territory. Berlin was no joke.

The bomber T for Tommy stood deserted in the dawn. Its crew strolled into the room. They made their way towards the table of a

WAAF officer, who pulled a large-scale map of the night's target area into view and began to question them quietly.

'Have a good trip?'

'Yes, thanks.'

'Get the target?'

'Oh, sure, sure, we got the target all right. Saw it right here.'

The finger of the bomb-aimer pointed to the map showing the capital of the Reich.

'Have any trouble?'

'Oh, not much.'

The crew was weary and their replies reflected this at first in monosyllabic, uninformative phrases. But under the influence of the WAAF's quiet manner, and the warmth and light after the darkness outside, they began to thaw out and relax. It was the section officer's job to steer them to tell their own experiences in their own way. By piecing together the stories of the bomb-aimer, the pilot, the tail-gunner navigator and the other members of the crew, she could write a concise and accurate report.

Eventually the last crew had been questioned, had filed out and gone to bed. Then the RAF intelligence officers collected the individual interrogation sheets, which gave them a consecutive narrative of the part played in the night's raid by the aircraft of the particular squadron.

Before leaving the behind-the-scenes WAAFs, the aircrews would want to spare a thought for the cooks who always had a meal ready on their return and had to meet such emergencies as 'Expect eighty extra for breakfast. They're arriving now!'

The time was 2.30am, and the WAAF catering officer of the Bomber Command station had just broken the glad tidings to the airwomen on night duty in the sergeants' mess that a squadron of Halifaxes coming back from a heavy raid on St Nazaire had been diverted to their station. Halifaxes were one of the mainstays in those days, and it was one of them that eighteen-year-old ACW Betty Campbell helped when in difficulty on its return from a raid on Germany.

A dark-haired, slightly built girl, Betty used to be a waitress in her hometown of Inverness, Scotland, and later in the WAAF served as a waitress in the officers' mess. Then she volunteered for the job of flare party work. This could be bitingly cold on the flying field at night or early morning, but she really felt in the front line helping the bombers. With two other girls, in charge of a corporal, Betty formed the flare party whose job was to assist the Aerodrome Control Pilot during the take-off and landing of aircraft.

The girls were stationed at each end of the runway during the take-off, connected to the ACP and Flying Control by telephone. They had to signal as each bomber became airborne and warn Flying Control of any obstruction. Sometimes a girl was posted at the intersection of two runways, so as to obviate any danger of collision in the dark between an aircraft taxiing from its dispersal point and another one taking off. The girls had the additional task of making sure that all landing lights were working properly, and in times of fog they lit the paraffin flares to help guide the pilots.

These WAAFs, with one of the most exciting jobs in the service, slept in a Nissen hut close to the control tower and were liable to be awakened before the scheduled return of the bombers. As soon as they were alerted, they had to leap out of bed, pull on their battledress and run to their posts. They had already proved themselves to the aerodrome control pilots and Flying Control officers, who praised them highly.

They seemed to thrive on excitement and emergency, and on this particular night the conditions were certainly set to provide one. The Halifaxes were on their way back to this northern aerodrome in the early hours, but landing conditions could hardly have been more foul. The clouds closed right in and a mist developed, making landing as awkward as bombing the target over Germany. Then one bomber circling the aerodrome asked for permission to land quickly as its petrol was running very low. Even as the message was being sent to Control, the wind suddenly veered round, and they had to recommend another runway.

This alternative runway had only just been lit, and the mist was thickening into a middle-of-the-night fog. Realizing the danger and difficulty the pilot might have in penetrating the mist to land on a runway only just lighted, Betty Campbell acted instantly. Loading an angle-of-glide indicator into a van, she rushed with it up the runway. She could not bear the thought of anything happening to the crew after getting so close to home.

This indicator was a heavy box-like contraption on four legs. Red, amber and green beams projected from it. If the pilot could see the red light, he knew he would under-shoot the runway; if he were approaching in the amber beam, he would over-shoot it; but if he could get the green light, he knew he was gliding in safely.

Betty and the van driver set up the indicator in record time. No sooner had they done so than the bomber came roaring down through the mist. Betty had heard it loudly; now she could see it as well. Thanks to her indicator, the pilot managed to make a fairly safe landing, but as he bumped to earth, he swerved slightly off the runway. The great Halifax thundered over the grass towards Betty and the driver. It came closer each second. They had to fling themselves face down on the sodden grass to avoid being struck by a wheel or a wing. But it missed them and came to a safe stop. The Flying Control officer complimented Betty for her prompt action.

Tragedies, such as the kind that a Stirling suffered when taking off with a full load of bombs, could and did happen so easily, landing at night in conditions like these. The bomber never got airborne at all, but crashed into two houses on the edge of the airfield and burst into flames. Section Officer Joan Marjorie Easton, from Eltham, Kent, raced out of her billet to the scene of the accident. Flight Sergeant Dobson of the New Zealand Air Force arrived there at the same time. Both of them knew that the bombs aboard the shattered Stirling were likely to explode at any second, but despite this they went to the cottages a few yards from the burning aircraft to warn the occupants of the danger and try to help them.

Then they entered one of the houses that had been struck by the plane and was actually alongside the blazing bomber. But while they were desperately trying to rescue the people inside, the inevitable happened. Set off by the scorching fire, one of the big bombs in the Stirling went off, and killed both of them. So Section Officer Easton and Flight Sergeant Dobson died for their service, as surely as if they had been in battle. Both were later mentioned in despatches, the highest honour they could have had posthumously, except the Victoria Cross.

An explosion with a less tragic outcome occurred at a bomb dump, which had to be closed. This happened one afternoon in the midst of preparations for a night's operations by the aircraft of that particular Bomber Command station. It looked as if one squadron would not be able to take off in its attack, because the bombs they should have carried were made inaccessible by the closure of the dump. Then the WAAF came to the aid. The transport officer organized a convoy of lorries, which set out for an airfield thirty miles away to bring back the necessary load of bombs. Even so, it was thought very unlikely that the borrowed bombs could be loaded, brought back to the airfield, unloaded and hoisted into the racks of the waiting aircraft in time for the take-off. Yet the drivers did their job so expertly and speedily that as soon as they arrived back at the home airfield, there was still a chance of being in time. So the WAAF drivers stripped off their tunics and helped the armourers to bomb up the aircraft. The bombers took off according to schedule and joined in the night's attack.

Next day, the transport drivers, including members of the WAAF, lined up in front of the transport officer and asked to be allowed to forfeit all days off and any leave due until the bomb dump could be opened again. So from early morning to late at night, the drivers not only carried out their normal duties, but also transported borrowed bombs and other appliances to replace those still unavailable. The squadron operated as though nothing had happened to its bomb dump.

This section of WAAF was one of two awarded the Sunderland Cup for the most efficient WAAF sections in Bomber Command. The cup was presented by the Mayor of Sunderland in memory of his son, killed with Bomber Command.

During 1944, the WAAFs had brought in safely more than twenty-five thousand aircraft in one bomber group, using the radio telephone. On one station alone, during the same year, more than a million telephone calls as well as a quarter of a million teleprinter messages were handled by WAAFs. In one group, too, WAAFs cooked and served some 50,000–60,000 meals a day, up to 5,000 at one station. And every time there was an operation, the motor transport section WAAFs of one Bomber Command group drove 12,000 miles, or 2 million miles a year.

At one Halifax Bomber group, the WAAFs undertook an unusual new duty. By manning the practice bombing ranges twenty-four hours a day, they released many men for other work. Part of their duty was to look after the lighting, and to replace indication marking after practice bombing runs.

But at least one more branch must be mentioned as vital to all airmen, especially bomber crews. This was composed of the girls who packed their parachutes: the girls on whom their lives literally depended.

The pilot nursed his bomber back towards Britain, the engine coughing in protest all the time. It was badly shot up; the German guns had been accurate. He felt glad the rest of his crew had baled out, because he knew now he would not make it. The plane was losing height: 1,000 feet, 750, 500 ... only feet between him and the earth now. He thought quickly. And what he thought was that he had better jump, though the chances must be much against his parachute pack opening in time.

'But it did, you know, and his life was saved. And we packed his parachute,' said an excited young WAAF, a veteran packer at twenty-two. She was one of the hundreds of girls on whose skill the safety of pilots hung, if they got into difficulties. Five hundred feet was terribly low. It showed the strength of the parachute used by the RAF. It showed, too, the minute care given by the girls to the great white umbrellas called packs.

At almost all RAF stations by 1942, the parachutes were packed and maintained by WAAFs. In the parachute room of a bomber station, the first thing to strike anyone was the pleasant warmth of the atmosphere. The temperature was never allowed to drop below 50 degrees, as the vital process of airing the parachutes went on here. The chutes always had to be bone dry, for the slightest damp would not only rot the silk as it was folded up in the pack, but it might delay the opening time – that paramount point in an emergency. If the pilot who baled out at 500 feet had had a damp pack, he would probably never have survived the fall. To be sure that no damp got into the parachute during continued operations, every member of aircrews had to bring their pack into the parachute room for airing once a month.

WAAFs kept a logbook of every parachute on the station. This book recorded airings, repairs, if ever used for a jump – in fact, the whole life history of the particular parachute. A parachute hung in the warm room for twelve hours, and then the WAAFs had the most responsible job of all – folding it up again ready for future use. Around the parachute room there were generally about a dozen chutes hanging airing from the ceiling, looking rather like a collection of tents whose guy ropes had been slackened.

If a parachute were ever used by aircrew to bale out, the WAAF who packed it was not forgotten afterwards. Just before a famous 1,000-bomber raid on Bremen, an excited young pilot rushed into the parachute room at an East Anglian bomber station, grabbed hold of an astonished fair-haired WAAF and shouted: 'Baby – you can surely pack a pack. Give me another – I'm off again!' It had been his first return to his own station since he had been picked up from the 'drink'. He had baled out and been adrift for ten hours. But the main thing was that his parachute had worked perfectly and the blonde WAAF had been its packer. Usually when they got back to their station, as in the case of this young flier, members of bomber crews who had baled out gave some small keepsake to the girl whose work had saved them.

Until it was examined closely, a parachute did not look as large as it was, with sixty-four square yards of pure silk in each one. They were composed in twenty-four triangles, each made of three pieces of silk, the seventy-two pieces each cut on the cross to give strength to the material. When they came in for airing it was the WAAFs duty to examine every square inch of the silk for possible flaws. So skilfully were the pieces of silk cut that they would resist a pressure of 400 pounds without tearing. And the cords connecting the silk with the pack were equally strong: twenty-four of them, all made of hundreds of strands of pure silk wound round and round together.

The all-important job of packing took an experienced girl half an hour per parachute. She worked at an enormous long bench on which she could stretch the chute full length. On the parachute, where each silk cord joined a seam, was a number, 1 to 24. In her left hand, the packer held number 13. She always started with number 13 to ensure getting an even number of folds each side. Nothing to do with superstition. Then she collected numbers 1 to 12 in her right hand and 13 to 24 in her left. The slightest mistake might twist the cords and mean a faulty opening. When she had finished folding, the parachute was triangular in shape ready to be folded in three and laced into the pack. Then the cords were collected up and folded into the pack, great care being taken to be sure that they did not twist or knot. They were kept in place by stout guards of webbing. If the ripcord were pulled, these guards automatically loosed as the silk blew free.

Learning to pack a parachute correctly took from two to four weeks, with extremely strict supervision because of the importance of the result. Little talking went on in the parachute room, for the girls knew that they must concentrate on the work every second. In every corner of Britain, WAAFs or 'Waffles' packed chutes for airmen. In the north, the damp climate and frequent rain brought their own special problems. The drying process had to be carried out more often.

In many RAF stations, the girls not only packed the parachutes, but also the complicated rescue dinghies which pilots took with them as part of their harness. Emergency rations in a watertight tin had to be included: barley sugar, chewing gum, malted milk tablets and energy tablets. Instructions for using the dinghy were printed in Polish, French, Czech and English. There had been a case of an indignant Dutch pilot who protested afterwards that he had been nearly drowned while he was trying to work out the instructions by a few words from each language!

Testing the dinghies was almost as intricate as testing the parachutes. They were inflated and left for twelve hours. Pressure tests were taken at regular intervals to make certain there was no slow puncture. The dinghies were entirely self-inflating as they opened, and if the rubber should perish they would be robbed of their buoyancy.

Another duty assumed by the WAAFs was caring for the dogs of flying crews. At one time it was quite common for the airmen to take their dog pets with them on operational flights, but then this became frowned on, and the animals had to stay patiently behind. An Aberdeen terrier taken on a typical bombing raid owed its life to the parachute packer, for the Flying Officer owning it took the dog along with him and had to bale out. Naturally he jumped with the dog in his arms. He told friends afterwards that the animal was much less scared than he was, and it fell asleep long before they completed their 5,000-feet fall! There was at least one dog, too, an Airedale, whose master would never return to claim him. The plane was shot down over the Ruhr, and although some of the crew was subsequently reported to be prisoners of war, their letters back to the squadron made it clear that the dog's master was dead. The WAAFs of the station held a draw to see who should take care of him, but it was finally decided that they should all share him, for the girl who won him found that the others were always feeding him and taking him for walks anyway. To the girls, the Airedale signified all the crews of Bomber Command who would never return.

Chapter 5

Angels of Mercy

The Hurricane pilot had completed his part in the fighter sweep over the French coast and was returning home towards his south-west England base. Speeding back over the Channel, at one of its widest points, he suddenly realized that his petrol was dangerously low and he might not have enough to reach home. As this dawned on him, the visibility was growing rapidly worse as well. Looking out at the murky air around him, and then at his gauges, he decided he would never make it, so he called up his operations room on the radiotelephone and explained: 'I'll have to bale out.'

WAAFs operating a radio-tender at the base specially to cope with such cases also received his call. At once, Corporal Margaret Lacey, of Netley, Southampton, replied by radio: 'Steer 170 degrees.'

The pilot heard the magic guidance, set his course and hoped for the best. On through the misty rain his Hurricane tore. They waited anxiously for his next report, and then it came: 'OK. I can see base now. I'll buy you a beer for this!'

The Hurricane lost height through the haze as the pilot strained to pick out the runway. In a minute or two he was down and the plane taxied slowly towards a dispersal point. As it reached there, the engine cut out. No petrol was left. It had been that close. The pilot jumped out of the cockpit with a grin and called to one of the ground crew caring for the Hurricane: 'That was a fine bit of work by those WAAFs. If it hadn't been for them, I'd probably be in a dinghy in the Channel and the kite at the bottom of the sea.'

He ran over to the radio-tender to thank the radiotelephone

operators for their prompt help. 'Damned good show!' But Margaret Lacey and her assistant, ACW Margaret Barrie, of Glasgow, thought very little special of it. They were glad they got him down safely, but it was all in the day's work. It was all done by radar – the modern miracle. No one was closer to radar than the WAAFs working under the topmost secrecy since 1939, who played such a vital role in the air victories achieved by radar.

Necessarily a silent service, theirs was also one of the most thrilling war jobs undertaken by women. They watched the slips on the cathode-ray tubes, indicating the approach of hostile aircraft over the Channel of the North Sea; they disseminated the warning of attack to defensive units throughout the country; they watched the progress of air battles at Ground Control interception stations; and later on they plotted the tracks of flying bombs and rockets.

Many lives of aircrew were saved by the constant watch of these girls, who frequently detected aircraft in distress and then guided them to an airfield by searchlight. They saw aircraft going down and passed on the exact position to Air Sea Rescue.

Another of the jobs undertaken by WAAFs working along the coast was to follow the movements of E-boats and other enemy shipping on their radar screens. They helped merchant vessels to keep to the channels swept clear of mines and guided them into safe waters. The Royal Navy's gratitude for radar help – and WAAF help – was reflected in a message from the Commander in Chief, The Nore, who said: 'Without the aid of the East Coast radar station, the warning of potential danger in the Nore Command waters would have been impossible, and much valuable tonnage might have been lost.'

WAAFs were just as vulnerable at some inland radar stations as those working under shellfire at Dover. Although they missed the glamour of other front-line service, for the very reason that their work was so secret, WAAF radar personnel received plenty of praise for their coolness and their technical efficiency.

Many of the coastal stations were really remote from civilization, and in the earlier days especially the girls had to walk miles to work at all hours of day and night, often through mud and snow. Many of them were trained to use and service some of the most delicate and complicated instruments ever invented – the radar apparatus developed in Britain for defensive and offensive use. Sir Robert Watson-Watt, pioneer of radar, said of the WAAF radar personnel: 'I have spoken of radar as the secret that was kept by a thousand women. This was a double understatement. There were more than a thousand of them, and they did vastly more than merely keep the secret. They were the front-line sentries of our air defence, and they applied to their brilliantly successful fulfilment of that task the qualities of acuteness of conscience, indomitable patience, keenness of perception, fineness of object, unquenchable enthusiasm, and calmness and steadfastness in danger. The work of the scientists who laid the foundations of radar would not have come to such full and timely realization without the contribution made by the women of the WAAF, who have so well served their country and the world.'

It was in November 1939 that twenty-six airwomen were selected for special duties. Radar was so secret at the time that the WAAF was not enrolled under such a classification. Yet at the peak of hostilities, there were over 4,000 officers and airwomen classified as radar signals officers, supervisors, mechanics and operators.

Ground control interception was the work of guiding patrolling fighters to the tails of enemy aircraft and putting the pilot close enough for him to 'see' the enemy on his own airborne radar set. From the beginning of the WAAFs' introduction to this work, it was apparent that they had a special aptitude. It soon became possible to release men from radar for overseas service in the same branch, and allow women to take over their duties in the last eighteen months of the war. Twenty-two WAAF officers became interception controllers and proved conspicuously successful.

Of the 5,000 flying bombs launched against this country during those later stages, very few escaped detection by radar, and credit was due and given to the WAAF operators for their vigilance and good temper, displayed under trying conditions. These WAAFs at radar stations in the line of fire hardly had an enviable job, for any of the missiles might have been – and frequently were – shot down on or near the coast, and crews off duty found it difficult to rest. Plotting grew fast and furious, followed as often as not by a violent rocking of the ops clock as flying bombs were brought down in the area.

The WAAFs by then had already shown the same spirit during the D-Day period, those at south-coast radar stations tracking the thousands of ships in that armada as they crossed the Channel; bombers attacking coastal batteries; gliders carrying paratroops and supplies; and fighters rendering air cover. It was reported that during the early hours of D-Day at one radar station the heat in the ops clock became so intense that to prevent the chinagraph pencils – used for marking maps – from melting, they had to be constantly dipped in water!

The WAAF radar operator worked with instruments so sensitive that the flight of a flock of geese could be detected. Usually, however, the girls had to track more ominous winged beings, whether Allied or enemy. They followed the big bomber formations going out to attack German targets night after night; they watched the telltale lines quivering and constantly changing shape in the cathode ray tubes as enemy bombers vibrated nearby; and their WAAF colleagues further inland – plotters, filterers, tellers and recorders – handled the information that they and the Royal Observer Corps fed back to them. The WAAFs were vital components of this vast and secret organization, which was one of the outstanding successes of the whole war.

Other backroom WAAFs with front-line jobs were the thousands of girls serving in Coastal Command. Each of them could claim to be part of the Battle of the Atlantic or the Battles of the Arctic, the North Sea or the Mediterranean. To the aircrews of Coastal Command belonged the credit for sinking U-boats and the safe arrival of convoys bringing food to Britain. To the WAAFs went the satisfaction of making their task easier. In nearly every section of Coastal, the girls shared the formidable duties of the RAF. Such highlights as the hunting of the *Bismarck* brought intensive and anxious work for the plotters who, with wireless operators, were once more in the picture during the rescue of the crew of a merchant vessel soon afterwards.

Coastal Command covered more mileage than any other major command, and their activities included operations as far away as the North African landings. These involved WAAF sparking-plug testers and workshop hands in some high-pressure work. At one station alone, the girls serviced over 6,000 sparking plugs during the fortnight.

Women radiotelephone operators of Coastal Command had duties just as serious as elsewhere, for they offered the only efficient means of communication between aircraft and shore. At a busy station far up north, where severe gales were all too common, the airwomen in Flying Control kept up ceaseless radio contact with squadrons returning after hours of flying in filthy conditions.

A typical emergency at this station for a girl keeping one of these night-long vigils happened when she intercepted a distress signal from a Liberator bomber returning through cloud and darkness, damaged and unsure of its position. The WAAF was able to tell the anxious pilot his whereabouts at once, and perhaps save the lives of the whole crew.

Always at one Coastal Command station or another, an aircraft was taking off or landing right round the clock and the calendar. For these planes more than any others flew on lone operations, long patrols lasting as many hours as the plane had fuel. Its destination could be an expanse of lonely sea; its aim reconnaissance or convoy escort. The navigator carried charts prepared by a WAAF maps clerk; equipment assistants had supplied the aircrews' kit; and parachute and dinghy packers guaranteed their safety gear. WAAF cooks had prepared the last meal before take-off and girl drivers taken them to dispersal point – the last visible link with home.

But by the medium of radio, the pilot remained in touch with his base. In the operations section, WAAF wireless operators awaited his signals, the first to hear of the sighting of a U-boat or an enemy vessel. They were ready for all emergencies, and if the pilot were forced to ditch, WAAFs were the link putting the air sea rescue into instant action.

WAAFs of Coastal Command and others were instrumental in saving the lives of several American aircraft in different ways. Leading Aircraftwoman Isabella Greig Leask, for instance, located a whole formation of American planes lost over Ireland. Her accurate location and identification enabled the RAF to make an interception and save no fewer than five planes and their crews, which might have run out of fuel. For this, Isabella was awarded the US Legion of Merit.

Another LACW, Peggy Grainger, of Portsmouth, rendered help to a USAAF aircraft in an even more direct emergency. When the plane crashed near Halton, Buckinghamshire, Peggy was one of the first on the scene. She at once gave first aid to Captain Carl GR Law, of Kirkersville, Ohio, who was burned and injured, but thrown clear of the crash. Peggy put out his burning clothes, improvised splints from branches of a nearby tree and tore up her own clothes to make dressings. Her resource certainly helped to save Captain Law's life, said the official citation of her conduct in a command routine order issued by Air Marshal Sir Arthur Barratt, Air Officer Commander in Chief of Technical Training Command, RAF. And for all Peggy knew, there might have been bombs in the burning aircraft.

Yet a third case of a WAAF helping American airmen in distress came when a Flying Fortress bomber crashed on an RAF airfield towards the end of the war. LACW Phyllis Day, from Kenton, Middlesex, was one of several WAAF drivers on a south coast airfield who, with the aid of jeeps, guided aircraft to their proper parking places. Phyllis was on duty this night, when thick fog hung over the whole area, a ghostly barrier between air and earth. The Fortress called up by radio to ask permission to make an emergency landing. It came in through the dark grey gloom, overshot the runway and could not pull up in time. It swerved, crashed into a parked plane and caught fire. Twenty-one-year-old Phyllis jumped into a jeep, accelerated sharply and raced right through the thick fog across the airfield to the scene.

Fierce flames pierced the fog. Live ammunition was exploding and bombs in the blaze seemed sure to go off at any second. Phyllis was first at the accident and by means of the portable radiotelephone in her jeep she passed back to Airfield Control valuable information enabling crash tenders and medical help to be sent in the least time. Despite the danger, Phyllis continued to direct rescue operations until the crash tender and ambulance arrived. Now help was on hand, but she did not stop, although the rescue personnel urged her to keep clear. She gave on-the-spot accounts of what further help would be needed in addition to the emergency aid already there.

Before finally leaving Coastal Command, another twenty-one-year-old girl must take special place in its record. A fascination for flying prompted LACW Mary Griffiths of Cymmer, near Port Talbot, to join the WAAF in 1942. In her first job as a balloon operator she did not get a chance to do more than watch the balloon flying, so she remustered to the trade of flight mechanic. Then this dark-haired, brown-eyed Welsh girl got the job after her own heart. She became the first WAAF to fly as a member of an aircrew with her commander-in-chief to the front. Mary was a flight mechanic of the Hudson aircraft belonging to Air Chief Marshal Sir Sholto Douglas, Air Officer Commanding in Chief of RAF Coastal Command.

As flight mechanic (airframes) she was responsible for everything except the engines of the aircraft, including changing the wheels. When the plane went on important missions, she always went with it, sitting in the second pilot's seat, next to Sir Sholto's personal pilot, Flight Lieutenant Eric Bland, DSO.

'I've never logged my flying hours,' Mary said, 'but I often wish I had kept a record, because I have done quite a lot of trips.' When the war was over, she planned to get married. Her fiancé was also a flight mechanic serving with the RAF.

Many other WAAFs took to the air, of course, during transit and for other purposes. At least one of them, the great golfer Pam Barton, was killed in an accident. But the branch with probably more operational flights to their credit than any other was the nursing orderly trade.

In March 1942 it had been agreed in principle to train WAAF nursing orderlies for duties with air ambulances. Volunteers were called for, and by June 1943, a year before D-Day, 214 of them had already been trained for such services. At this time, they were used only in Britain, where they travelled with, and looked after, sick or injured personnel being flown by air to hospital, or from one hospital to another. The WAAF proved particularly valuable in this work between the scattered Scottish islands and the mainland, where air was virtually the only transport possible for urgent cases.

More exciting duties lay in store for them, however, and in March 1944 the Air Council approved their use in connection with the forthcoming invasion of Europe, to escort casualties from the battle areas by aircraft back to Britain. It was realized that this work would mean hardship and danger, but the effect on the wounded men would be very valuable, in addition to the practical aspect of freeing men for other service. Volunteers came forward. These girls were included in the crews of transport aircraft, not ambulances, to operate a freight shuttle service in the Normandy battle zone.

That same month of March, 76 WAAF nursing orderlies were posted to casualty air evacuation duties in Transport Command, ready to undertake this work. The aircraft were ready and waiting, and when D-Day came they would take out freight and bring back the wounded.

Within a week of D-Day, the WAAFs were in Normandy. From an advanced landing strip on Tuesday 13 June, D+7, came news of the first WAAF medical orderlies to land in France. Soon after sunrise, three Dakotas of Transport Command descended on the strip, and out of each one stepped a WAAF nursing orderly. None of these girls had been out of Britain before that day. They made their first entry into the Continent in style, with an escort of Spitfires. They were greeted with gun flashing from further inland, while over to the east they spotted a bombing attack in progress on enemy positions, with flak-bursts littering the morning sky.

Like everyone else on this advanced airfield, they were in danger from enemy snipers. Most of the sniping nests had been cleared up, but over in a village nearby – closely surrounded by trees – snipers still operated from concealed spots. The girls heard how three men had been shot at the airfield on the previous night, while working on the runway. They watched armed parties, carrying stretchers, going out in Indian file to search out the enemy.

They could not be closer to war than this, yet whatever the emotions the girls were feeling, they kept them well disciplined. As soon as they alighted, they went straight to the ambulances, which were waiting with the wounded at the edge of a cornfield. The WAAFs took along a hamper containing flasks of tea.

'Blimey! Women!' shouted an Army engineer as he saw them approaching, and the gen soon spread among the soldiers and airmen that there were girls on the camp. Heads popped up over hedges and little groups of dusty soldiers with rifles or spades gathered to watch them carry on with their work. The girls were wearing smart blue battledress blouse and trousers with a Red Cross on white armlets to indicate their mission. All three had previous nursing experience. Corporal Lydia Alford (aged twenty-seven) of Eastleigh, Hants, used to be an assistant nurse in a hospital; LACW Edna Birkbeck (twenty-five) of Wellingborough, Northants, was in the civil nursing service before she joined the WAAF; and LACW Lyra Roberts of Lake Vyrawy, Shropshire, had been a hospital nurse.

It was still early morning when the aircraft landed and the girls' first concern was to see that the wounded were warm. They tucked blankets around the stretchers and held welcome cups of tea to the lips of the men who were unable to help themselves.

A thin yellow dust deeply covered these Normandy fields, and the wind blowing in from the sea swept it up in choking clouds. Later in the morning Spitfires began to land in quick succession, and as each sped along the wire mesh runway the dust was whirled up and completely obliterated the airfield. The girls held blankets as screens for the men who were lying or sitting on the grass beside the ambulances.

Normally the freight, which the Dakotas had brought over, could have been unloaded and the wounded men put aboard within twenty minutes. But the weather forecast was bad today. The girls had been allowed to attend the briefing back in England before the dawn take-off, and they had heard how a front was sweeping in from the east, bringing with it low cloud and mist. Permission could not be given for the three planes to return to England until visibility improved.

By early afternoon a signal was received that the first Dakota could leave. Meanwhile the nurses had been trying to cheer the men and make them comfortable. They went from one to another, saying, 'It won't be long now. We'll soon have you home.' They refilled the flasks with tea from an army bivouac and kept the wounded warm.

Word came through that there was a chance of take-off. The stretchers were taken out of the ambulances and swiftly transferred to the planes, fitted up with racks to receive them. Then the order was cancelled. Visibility over the Channel was now nil, it seemed. All the stretchers had to be taken out again because it was felt that the grounded aircraft would be targets for any enemy bombers that might come over. The girls had to cheer the disappointed men.

At last one Dakota was allowed to leave, with the slightly wounded: the sitting cases who could help themselves if the plane had to come down in the sea. Corporal Alford went in this aircraft. She propped up the wounded leg of a Canadian soldier with her parachute pack, and throughout the bumpy flight – through an opaque sea mist all the time – she went from one to another as the Dakota lurched from side to side, offering tea; easing the bandages of a man who had a bad sniper wound in his arm and was in pain; talking to shell-shock cases.

The other two aircraft had to wait until early evening before the weather improved. The remaining two orderlies, sustaining themselves with hard biscuits and tea, stayed beside the wounded all the time, except for one brief interval when they were taken around the camp in a jeep and picked up a couple of German helmets and a gas mask as souvenirs. They called on a farm where the farmer's daughter ran out to pick them a bunch of flowers.

At last the signal came through that they could leave. The planes took off amid clouds of dust. LACW Roberts had a serious stretcher case aboard – a soldier with a chest wound. She had to administer oxygen to him most of the way.

The girls' hair was thick with dust, and their clothes yellowed with it, when they got back to base. They looked tired – but happy. Now that the ambulance service to the RAF landing strip had started, it would operate whenever the weather was favourable, taking back the more serious cases.

Another flying nurse was twenty-one-year-old LACW Helen Venter, once a nurse at Redhill County Hospital in Surrey. Her husband, a pilot, was missing after the famous Augsburg raid, and so she volunteered for this special invasion duty for the sake of his memory.

Since that day so soon after the Normandy landings, more than 50,000 casualties were flown home from European battle areas by the end of the year. About 180 WAAFs were employed on this air evacuation. Seventy of these girls were actually nursing orderlies on flying duties and forty worked in Casualty Air Evacuation Centres. The rest acted as ambulance drivers and ward waitresses. Three-quarters of the nursing orderlies had completed forty flights, regarded as the equivalent to an operational tour, by December 1944. This involved 200 operational flying hours each. They were the Angels of Mercy.

Chapter 6

Special Operations Executive

Told now for the first time are the authentic accounts of all the gallant girls of the British Women's Auxiliary Air Force who were dropped into Europe to work for the famous Special Operations Executive. Fourteen WAAFs went out. Only eight returned. Five were killed in concentration camps and one died of illness.

These are their names: Noor Inayat Khan, Diana Hope Rowden; Cecily Margot Lefort; Beatrice Yvonne Cormeau; Yolande Elsa Maria Beekman; Cecile Pearl Cornioley; Anne Marie Walters; Yvonne Jeanne Therese de Vibraye Baseden; Maureen Patricia O'Sullivan; Lilian Verna Rolfe; Muriel Tamara Byck; Phyllis Ada Latour; Sonia Esmee Florence Butt; Christine Granville.

This is their story.

Three girls shared the distinction of being the first WAAFs to land in France, all in June 1943. They were Diana Rowden, Cecily Lefort and the immortal Madeleine, Noor Inayat Khan. Madeleine's life has already been told, so it is sufficient to say that after being betrayed in Paris for about 75 francs, she was taken to the hated Gestapo headquarters in Avenue Foch in Paris, thence to the civil prison of Pforzheim, in chains. In September 1944, after ten months in Pforzheim, she was suddenly summoned and escorted to a railway station, where she met two other British women agents. They did not know it, but their journey would be brief. Their destination was Dachau. There, on the morning of 15 September 1944, they were led out of their cells and shot in the back of the head. Their bodies were immediately cremated. Noor Inayat Khan was posthumously awarded the George Cross and the Croix de Guerre.

Diana Rowden was born on 31 January 1915, to British parents, and educated in both England and France. A freelance journalist before the war, she spoke fluent French, Italian and Spanish. She also had administrative experience in France early in the war while working with the French Red Cross and the Anglo-American Ambulance Corps attached to the British Expeditionary Force. She succeeded in escaping from France after Dunkirk by her own devices.

Diana returned to Britain in September 1941, joined the WAAF about Christmas and worked in the Air Ministry as a section officer on intelligence duties. But being anxious to return to France and work against the Germans at closer quarters, she volunteered for Special Operations Executive in March 1943.

Then followed an arduous time of training: parachute jumping, field craft, map reading, and most of all, security, for the safety of a whole group might depend on her ability to tell a plausible story if stopped unexpectedly by the Gestapo. After completing this training, which all the girls undertook, Diana was landed in France by Lysander aircraft. Her cover name was Juliette Therese Rondeau and her pseudonym Paulette. Her mission: to act as courier to a British liaison officer of the Stockbroker circuit, working in the Jura.

Diana and the circuit's radio operator became installed in the sawmill of M Pauly in Clairvaux and they soon set up radio contact with London. But a month after their arrival, the Germans arrested their commanding officer. Other arrests in the same area followed, which seriously compromised Diana and the radio operator, yet for four months she worked untiringly, travelling long distances in dangerous territory to keep up the links between the various groups of the circuit. During this period, the Gestapo was constantly looking for the two of them, and then the inevitable happened.

On 18 November the Germans arrested them both. The very next day, moreover, another woman agent, Miss Vera Leigh, FANY, was denounced and arrested. Miss Leigh had landed two days before Diana and was a courier between Paris and the region of the River Yonne. Vera was detained in Fresnes prison, Paris, where yet a third woman was already confined. She was Miss A Borrel, actually the first girl to make an operational parachute jump. This Frenchwoman had landed in Brittany on 24 September 1942, and was caught with a British officer on 25 June 1943.

Diana Rowden herself was taken to various prisons in or near Paris until May 1944, when she found herself in Fresnes. On 13 May 1944, these three women, together with five others arrested while engaged on similar work, were all transferred to Karlsruhe city gaol for women in the Riefstahlstrasse. It is not known precisely why they were sent there, but the Karlsruhe Gestapo were instructed by the Reichssicherheitshauptamt Berlin (RSHA, the headquarters of the Gestapo) to take delivery of the eight women and hold them there.

The arrival of the girls caused considerable disturbance for the prison was only a civilian gaol and had no facilities for guarding political prisoners. Eventually, a teleprint message concerning four of the eight women was received by the head of the Karlsruhe Gestapo telling him to arrange for their execution in a convenient camp. Natzweiler was chosen.

Between 4 and 5.30am on 6 July 1944, with the Allies advancing in Normandy, Miss Borrel, Miss Leigh, Diana Rowden and an unidentified fourth girl were conducted to Natzweiler, by large car. Their two guards saw the camp commandant Hatjenstein and various other officials, handing over with the women a copy of the movement order and the Vollzugszettel – the execution order – received from Berlin. This did not specify why, where or how the execution was to take place. Natzweiler had apparently been chosen simply because it was the most convenient concentration camp to Karlsruhe, although it was one for men only.

None of the Gestapo involved took any steps to find out whether the four girls had been tried and legally condemned to death, nor to acquaint them with their impending fate. In fact, it is clear that the Gestapo men were fully aware that there had been no legal proceedings and the girls were not under sentence of death. Yet the orders were accepted without question.

On the journey to Natzweiler, the girls were told that they were on their way to a camp where they would do agricultural work. The pitiful little party reached Natzweiler at about 3 o'clock on the afternoon of 6 July 1944. Natzweiler was a low-hutted camp set high among dark trees on a mountainside. A single straight road led up to the hutments. Lower down the road stood the gas chamber and the Hotel du Struthol, three storeys high plus attics. As the girls walked from the gate down the camp road to the administrative offices, a number of the male prisoners saw them clearly, and again as they were being taken from there to the bunker – the prison within the camp. Their presence quickly became known and widely discussed. The inmates somehow learnt that they were British and French. Lieutenant Commander O'Leary and a Belgian, Dr Boogaerts, managed to make brief contact with two of the girls whose cells faced the infirmary.

As evening approached, the other prisoners realized that something sinister had been planned. The Germans ordered all prisoners to be in their huts by 8pm behind blacked-out windows. No one saw the girls after that. Between 9.30 and 10.30pm they were taken out singly from the bunker cells to the crematorium. Even at the last, when one of the girls asked why she was being injected, they told her it was an inoculation against typhus. Whether or not they all became unconscious is open to doubt, but what is certain is that immediately after the injection they were cremated.

The Germans' plea that all concerned were only anxious to act as humanely as possible collapses since no one took any steps to safeguard the girls' legal rights, and the doctor did not even consider it necessary to ascertain what drug he was injecting. The doctor, Rohde, was subsequently sentenced to death for the murder of the four girls. Four other Germans received periods of imprisonment ranging from four to thirteen years, and the camp commandant Hartjeostein got a life sentence.

For her services, Diana Rowden was recommended for the MBE, but in view of her death could only be awarded a posthumous mention in despatches. She was also recommended for the Croix de Guerre.

Cecily Lefort was considerably older than Diana. Born in Britain on 30 April 1900, Cecily married a French doctor practising in Paris. Before the war, she acted as his receptionist. She was taken on by SOE in January 1943 and after training she received an honorary commission in the WAAF on 15 May 1943. A month and a day later she was in a Lysander over France.

Her documents had been made out in the name of Cecil Marguerite Legrand, and her SOE pseudonym was Alice. Cecily landed safely and contacted a reception committee organized by a British lieutenant colonel known as Roger, commanding the Jockey circuit. Roger was busy building his organization in this area of the Drome, Vaucluse and Bouches de Rhône departments near the Mediterranean.

In this wide-flung region, Cecily took her place as his courier, carrying messages and orders to the distant section leaders under his command in the southeast of France. She always kept cool when passing enemy police controls on her routes.

With work like this, the unexpected could always be expected. On 15 September 1943, Cecily was spending the night in the 'safe house' owned by L Gaujat in Montelimar. Suddenly a detachment of the Gestapo, from their St Etienne headquarters, arrived and thrust their way into the house. Seizing and searching Cecily's handbag, they came across a compromising document. On the spur of the moment, she could offer no plausible explanation for it – because there could be none. They took her away for further questioning. It was believed that Gaujat's safe house must have been betrayed by one of his personal enemies working for the Germans. Luckily Gaujat himself escaped through a window at the rear of the house when the Gestapo arrived.

Nothing more was heard of Cecily for nearly two years, when in the summer of 1945 inmates of the Frauenkonzentrations-lager Ravensbrück, near Fürstenberg in Mecklenburg, were saved by the Swedish Mission and taken to Stockholm. According to these witnesses, Cecily underwent an operation, successfully carried out by the camp's surgeon, Dr Treitel. For two of three months after that, she continued to receive better food, but could not regain her strength. In November or December 1944, the Jugendlager was opened nearby, supposed to be a convalescent home for inmates from the notorious main camp. The Germans made it known that prisoners transferred there would not have to work, which naturally appealed to many of them, since all were in a state of extreme weakness. Cecily was transferred to the Jugendlager in January 1945.

The true significance of the 'convalescent' camp soon became known, however, and word got back to the main camp that women went for convalescence were generally gassed or killed by a lethal injection if they did not make a quick recovery. As soon as this was realized, the French leader of the women interned in the main camp got a message through to the British and French women in the Jugendlager urging them to volunteer for work and return to the main camp. Only two acted on this advice. Cecily and another woman were considered too weak for work by the Germans and kept back at the Jugendlager. Cecily was killed by lethal injection and cremated in early March 1945, with the war in Europe reaching its last stages.

On 14 September 1945, one month before news of her death came through, Cecily had been recommended for the MBE. And so, like the legendary Madeleine, Diana Rowden and Cecily Lefort both died, and none of that brave trio who were dropped into France on 16 June 1943 ever returned home. And three of the remaining eleven WAAFs parachuted into France were to die before victory was won.

Beatrice Cormeau had good reason to hate the Germans. Her husband had been killed on active service in November 1940. So when she joined the WAAF as an ACW/a on 4 October 1941, she was a widow with a young daughter.

Before the war Beatrice had attended the Queen Street Ladies College in Edinburgh and spoke French, German and Spanish. She had lived mostly in Brussels working as secretary to a British barrister and international lawyer. Early in 1943 her languages and other qualifications singled her out as especially suitable for service in SOE and she was asked if she would like to volunteer.

The conflict she had to resolve was one between a mother's love for her five-year-old daughter and the help she could be to the Allied cause. Beatrice decided that in the long run she would be doing more for her child by volunteering for SOE work in France. She remembered how the Germans had broken up her family life. Accordingly on 22 August 1943, with the pseudonym of Annette, she was parachuted as W/T operator to join the Wheelwright circuit near Bordeaux in southwest France. A British officer known simply as Colonel Hilaire commanded this particular circuit.

From the very moment she started work, it became clear that Beatrice was one of the most technically efficient wireless operators yet sent into the field. The remarkable thing, moreover, was that she maintained the high standard throughout her whole service of over one year. Month after month, she enciphered and sent some 400 W/T messages without once being caught, although her positions were detected more than once. The W/T traffic from London she received mostly at night and then deciphered; this amounted to an even greater number of messages.

It was this dependability of Beatrice's over a long period that formed the basis of establishing Hilaire's circuit as one of the largest and most effective in all France. In fact her correct transmission of W/T traffic enabled no fewer than 135 successful parachute operations to be carried out in the area during the vital time from October 1943 to September 1944.

The arms and explosives, as well as other equipment received as a result, completely transformed the Maquis. From a group living mostly in the forests and merely mounting ambushes and sabotage operations they became a real fighting force that could and did give valuable help to the advancing Allied armies during and after the invasion.

Since the German radio location service never stopped searching for clandestine transmitting sets, Beatrice was compelled to move her equipment frequently, often travelling as much as sixty kilometres a day to do so, sometimes through German control points. Generally she tried to work from isolated farmhouses situated so that she should have ample warning of anyone approaching the area. The strain of such a life, coupled with the nomadic existence it involved, naturally told on her nerves, yet she never complained nor asked for relief.

D-Day came and went. After the landings, she was concerned in many actions with German troops, continuing to transmit and receive messages by day and night, despite the enemy now being really near. At the battle of Castelnau, Beatrice carried her radio set actually through the enemy lines under fire and transmitted her vital W/T messages to the home station in England from a roadside farmhouse. Again, at the battle of Lannemezan, she showed the courage by then expected of her when she continued with her duty while under machine-gun fire and air bombing. The losses inflicted on enemy divisions passing through that area were largely due to the superb service she gave her commanding officer.

With the Americans driving swiftly northward after the Riviera landings, south-west France was soon liberated, and Beatrice, too, could be freed to return to England on 25 September 1944. After visiting her daughter, her first thought was to get back into harness and do any more work she could for the cause near her heart. Beatrice furthered Anglo-French relations in various ways during the next months, by now having achieved the rank of flight officer.

In February 1945 she was presented to HM the Queen Mother, together with other WAAF officers who had rendered outstanding war services, and she signed off in SOE on July 9. For her work she was awarded the MBE, while the French recognized her heroism with the Croix de Guerre avec Palme.

Just a few weeks after Beatrice Cormeau had landed safely in south-west France, Section Officer Yolande Beekman had a less-organized reception. Born in Paris of Swiss parents, Yolande came to England in 1929, and so spoke English with a slight accent. More important, though, she spoke French without any trace of foreign influence. Before the war, Yolande and her mother ran a business in London as children's modistes. Then, together with her two sisters, Yolande joined the WAAF, where she enrolled as ACW 2004266. She moved to SOE in February 1943 and was commissioned and promoted section officer in the April of 1943. She married Sergeant J Beekman whom she met during her W/T training courses for SOE.

Once more the stage was prepared for a WAAF officer to be dropped into France. Under the cover name of Yolande Chauvigny, and with her pseudonym of Pariette, she found herself in the familiar lonely Lysander on 17 September 1943. Her role: W/T operator to the Musician circuit under the command of Canadian officer Guy, the name by which he was known.

She landed safely enough near Tours, but no reception committee could meet her there to help her reach the goal of St Quentin. Yolande took the only possible decision in the circumstances – to travel alone from Tours right through Paris to St Quentin. With her all the way on this very public journey went her secret radio transmitter, disguised as a suitcase: a perilous trip in view of the strict system of enemy controls in force.

For four months, Yolande continued to carry out her hazardous duties as ciphering and W/T operator for her commanding officer, who had created a large Resistance organization in the Lille–St Quentin area. She transmitted regularly three times a week to England and on at least two occasions changed her place of work. Through Major Guy's and Yolande's efficiency, the Resistance forces were able to receive arms and explosives parachuted to suitable spots at night.

But on 15 January 1944, near St Quentin, whilst actually in the process of transmitting from the Cafe du Moulin Brule (or an adjoining house, no one will ever know), Yolande and her commanding officer were both arrested by the Gestapo. The Germans took them first to the Gestapo prison at 84 Avenue Foch in Paris, later transferring them to the Fresnes prison. It was later learned that the Germans had been trying for a long time to find out the location of Yolande's secret transmitter, as enemy D/F-ing cars had been seen in the vicinity. Unluckily, her W/T set, the crystals and codes were also captured by the Germans, which had the most tragic results later on. From the interrogation of Germans, imprisoned after the war, it was established that on 12 May 1944 Yolande was one of the eight British women including Diana Rowden who were taken from Fresnes to Karlsruhe. Once there, they were separated and placed in the civilian jail for women, each sharing cells with one or two German women, in most cases also political prisoners.

The woman who shared Yolande Beekman's cell and befriended her testified that the eight English girls were not ill treated while in the Karlsruhe jail. The news of the Normandy landings percolated through to them, buoying up their morale. And they never lost courage or faith during the heavy Allied air raids on the city.

On the afternoon of 11 September 1944, Yolande and two of the other girls were warned by the head wardress to prepare to leave, and the Germans returned their personal belongings to them. During the night they were handed over to two Gestapo officials, who when subsequently arrested by the Americans completed the story of Yolande Beekman. The Gestapo men drove the three girls by car to the station, where they boarded a train to Munich. Here they changed into a local train to Dachau, some 20 miles north west of Munich, arriving late in the evening. They had to walk to the dreaded camp, which they finally reached about midnight. The girls were at once locked up in cells, apparently unaware of what would happen next, for they had travelled in ordinary compartments of the trains and seemed glad to have the chance of seeing each other again. They chatted eagerly in English.

Between 8 and 10 next morning, 13 September 1944, the three girls were taken out of their cells and shot through the back of the head. Their bodies were immediately cremated. One of them, of course, was Madeleine – Noor Inayat Khan. For her services in France, Yolande Beekman was awarded a mention in despatches and also recommended for the Croix de Guerre.

Before she became Mrs Cornioley, Pearl Witherington formed and led a whole Maquis group with her husband-to-be as second command. When war broke out, Pearl was working in the Paris Embassy as secretary to the air attaché. She left the capital where she had been born and managed to make her way to Lisbon by March 1941, arriving in Britain in July.

For a while, Pearl served as personal assistant to the director of Allied air co-operation and foreign liaison at the Air Ministry. But then she volunteered for special service in France and was seconded to SOE on 8 June 1943. Three months' training and she was ready to be parachuted into occupied territory. Actually, the RAF made two abortive attempts to drop her – bad weather interfered with the plans each time. Finally Pearl parachuted at the dead of the night of

22–23 September. The weather was still not good on that night, and a high wind blew her away from the agreed landing ground. Eventually she contacted the reception committee huddled in a remote field to meet her, but her luggage, which had also been parachuted, could not be found.

She was escorted safely to Chateauroux, where she boarded a train for Limoges. Before leaving England, Pearl had been given the cover of a secretary in the Société Allumetière Française, under the name of Genevieve Touzalin. She was supposed to be employed in Marseilles and had an identity card for that town. She kept this cover without much trouble until November.

Then with the complicity of the secretary of the mairie in the small village of Montant Les Cremaux in the Gers, she succeeded in obtaining registered papers in the name of Marie Jeanne Marthe Verges, a girl who had disappeared. Further papers Pearl was able to acquire purported to show that she was working for the firm Isabelle Lancray, manufacturing cosmetics, as 'chef de service commerciale'. This fresh identity enabled her to move around freely. She also had a contact in the firm whom she had known before the war and who would have vouched for her in case of arrest. Pearl successfully kept this cover throughout the rest of her mission.

And what of her mission? She was to act as courier to the powerful circuit known as Shipwright in south-western France, under a British officer with the code name of Hector. Pearl had the additional task of acting as liaison officer with a Resistance group who had a large number of men in the Maquis, commanded by a French colonel. Pearl managed to make contact with these men and collaborated with a sabotage group, which tried to put the Michelin works in Clermont Ferrand out of action. The effort failed due to lack of sabotage instruction at that time in this region.

London recalled Hector for consultations about future activities and a Lysander plane picked him up on 15 October. He had been due to remain in England for only a fortnight, but due especially to bad weather he could not return until 23 January 1944. During his absence, Pearl was not idle. She widened her circle of contacts and personally started courses of sabotage instruction, with good results.

She also helped with transportation and installation of Eureka equipment designed to aid pilots in locating the dropping grounds for their special operations. The work was difficult and dangerous, due to the bulky nature of the gear.

If found by the Germans, it would have been quite impossible to explain away the Eureka equipment. All this work involved not only mental but physical strain, which began to tell on Pearl. She kept going till Hector returned to the sector, but then she fell seriously ill with neuralgic rheumatism, brought about by long nights in cold trains. For in spite of attempts by Pearl and her various friends, she had been unable to find a secure room to live in until about Christmas time, and so had spent most of her nights in trains, mainly between Clermont Ferrand, Toulouse and Chateauroux.

Soon after her return to work, Hector and his W/T operator were arrested at Montlucon. This proved a heavy blow to their whole organization, as well as the inevitable personal tragedy of friends in the hands of the Gestapo. But Pearl did not waver and undertook a hazardous journey to warn other British missions about the arrests. Immediately she had got back again to Montlucon, the Germans surrounded the town searching for other Resistance leaders. Together with two other officers, however, Pearl escaped through the German lines to St Gaultier, where they could send a W/T message to London asking that the BBC should broadcast a general warning to lie low in view of the attempts to make further arrests.

Pearl was now on the run with Henri Cornioley, but the weather improved as spring blossomed. They moved to La Chatre and other places, finally setting up a headquarters again at Dun-le-Poelier in the Nord Indre department. They moved to the guardhouse of the Chateau des Souches, the owners there receiving them eagerly – despite the danger they all knew they were running.

On the eve of D–Day, the BBC broadcast the 'Action' messages in conventional phrases previously agreed, and Pearl assumed command in this Nord Indre area, with Henri acting as her number two. In accordance with the Action orders, she formed a small Maquis of peasants who volunteered, installing them in the outhouses of the old chateau.

But on 11 June 2,000 Germans attacked them at 8am. The small Maquis of some forty men, badly armed and scarcely yet trained, put up a fierce fight, helped by the neighbouring community Maquis of a hundred men. The battle went on all day, ending only as the summer dusk fell at 10pm. In the fourteen hectic hours, the Germans lost eighty-six men against the Maquis casualties of twenty-four, including civilians and wounded, whom the Germans killed off. Another blow was the loss of the Eureka and S-phone equipment captured by the Germans. The enemy also set fire to the surrounding farms in this lovely country area. As a result of the attack, the whole area rapidly became so unhealthy for any future Maquis operations that Pearl had to remove the remnants of her group to another part of the country. From the very next day, 12 June, she established her HQ for ten weeks at Doulcay par Maray, Loir et Cher. But even here the Germans were close on her heels, forcing her to spend every night in woods near the town.

The Normandy beachhead was well established by now but any diversions that Pearl and all her fellow operators throughout France could contrive would be valuable in weakening enemy resistance. So Pearl radioed a request to London for a parachute drop of arms to her new sector. The first one of these was successfully organized on 24 June, followed at short intervals by no fewer than twenty-two other drops. The equipment that fell to them from the night sky helped to rearm her Maquis men.

These parachute drops in the area were very difficult to arrange, however, as German observation posts were scattered liberally over the region. Since D-Day, moreover, the enemy had been more alert than ever for activity of this kind. It was out of the question, of course, to organize day drops, or to light guiding fires for drops during the non-moon periods. In spite of all these handicaps, Pearl lost only one parachute operation – and this was an accident in no way her own fault. One of the containers loaded with hand grenades floated down to earth but burst on impact with the ground. Explosions stuttered and spattered over the night air. There was nothing to do but try to get away. But the Germans traced the fields, got the material and slew four Maquisards.

Pearl's greatest difficulty in regrouping and organizing the Maquis at this time was the absence of a military chief who had to be a Frenchman. This was remedied in July, however, by the arrival of Commandant Francis and his deputy, Capitaine Bourguignon, who took over command and the task of training the men. The boost to morale of the D–Day landings had been so great that by 27 July Pearl's Maquis band had grown to 1,500 men.

Pearl was invariably in the forefront of the fighting, which became more and more frequent and on a larger scale. By numerous ambushes and attacks on unwary Germans and their column, her Maquis killed over 1,000 enemies and wounded many times that number. The whole group snowballed to substantial military proportions, so that it was also able to assist in effecting the surrender of 18,000 Germans in the Issoudun area, who were handed over to the advancing American troops at Orleans. Her group received the special thanks from Allied Headquarters for having also provided the intelligence on the exact whereabouts of sixty German armoured trains steaming from Strasbourg to Normandy to try and repulse the Allied advance there. These supply trains never reached their destination, as they were destroyed en route by attacks from the air.

Pearl completed her mission magnificently and married Lieutenant Henri Cornioley on 25 October 1944. After returning to England, she was sent back to France on a goodwill tour with other SOE officers to convey thanks to all the patriotic French men and women who had risked their lives to help SOE in the joint effort to free France. Pearl received the MBE for her services and the Croix de Guerre avec Palme en Bronze. Flight Officer Pearl Cornioley was demobilized on 30 April 1945 – the date of Hitler's death – but reappointed the following January to an honorary commission in the WAAF to be sent to the USA on a speaking mission.

Two of the youngest SOE girls were Anne Marie Walters and Yvonne Baseden, aged only sixteen and seventeen when war broke out.

Anne Marie was born in Geneva and had been a student in 1939. She eventually joined the WAAF as LACW 2001920 and due to her fluency in French was taken over by SOE in June 1943. After being trained as a W/T operator and promoted assistant section officer,

Anne was parachuted into France on 4 January 1944, with another British officer. Her pseudonym was Colette and they were posted to the Wheelwright circuit, commanded by the British officer known as Colonel Hilaire, to act as a courier.

This circuit was one of the largest in the country, covering the area from Vierson to the Pyrenees, and centred around Toulouse. Anne Marie had an authentic identity card registered in Auch by Colonel Hilaire, who was extremely powerful in that region. In the course of her courier duties, Anne Marie had to travel to the different sectors of the circuit by any means of transport available: bus, train, taxi and often bicycle. Three trips took her to zones as widely apart as the Dordogne, Lot et Garonne, Gers, Hautes Pyrenees and Hauts Garonne, carrying London's orders to the various regional chiefs under Hilaire's command. Her messages included BBC warning and action orders prior to D-Day.

In the rugged Pyrenees sector, Anne Marie helped set up arms depots, carried explosives to wherever these were specifically needed and also found time to escort some British and French officers who had escaped from the Eysse prison, in Lot et Garonne, to their escape line contacts for transit across the Spanish border.

D+1. On 7 June, Colonel Hilaire and his staff took to the Maquis. They occupied Castelnau-sur-l'Auvignon, near Condon (Gers). He and his 1,500 Maquisarde held this for a vital fortnight, until the Germans attacked them on 21 June with a formidable force of nearly 2,000 men, enemy soldiers who could ill be spared from the main battlefronts of Europe. Anne Marie was present at this battle, which lasted six bloody hours, and resulted in 380 enemy casualties, 247 of whom were killed. The village was razed to the ground.

After this encounter, Hilaire and his staff had to withdraw having blown up their ammunition dump. The remaining men joined up with the Maquis of Panjas, later transformed into the Bataillon d'Armagnac. Another week passed and then, on 29 June, Anne Marie was a member of the reception committee to which a Jedburgh team from Algiers was dropped by parachute. Jedburgh teams generally consisted of a British, an American and a French officer, with their own W/T operator. Their arrival acted as a great morale lifter. Anne Marie carried out liaison between this fresh team and Colonel Hilaire, mainly on her bicycle, a trusty if rusty friend.

A month later, on 28 July, Colonel Hilaire decided to send Anne Marie to London with a full report on the local situation. She started off on August 1 over the Pyrenees with three American pilots who had been shot down over Europe, a Dutchman and two other men. After losing their way four times in the treacherous country, they finally climbed the Pic du Gard, passed near Boutx and Melle and on 4 August reached Lerida, where the party was delayed for over a fortnight by the Spanish authorities.

On 23 August Anne Marie succeeded in reaching Barcelona, then on to Madrid and Gibraltar, where she got a ship back to Britain, arriving in September. She was so keen on continuing her work that she did two further practice parachute jumps 'just to keep her hand in'.

But Colonel Hilaire's region had already been liberated by this time, so there was no need to send her back. Anne Marie was signed off on 1 October 1944 and awarded the MBE. She became Madame Anne Marie Comert, and lived in Paris.

Seventeen-year-old Yvonne Baseden could not know what lay ahead of her while she was working as a secretary in a British industrial firm in the first year of the war. At the age of eighteen and a half, Yvonne Jeanne Therese de Vibraye Baseden – to name her fully – volunteered for the WAAF, where she soon reached the rank of section officer. Then followed the familiar transfer to SOE, where her bilingual French on her mother's side could be better used. After training as a W/T operator and promotion to flight officer, Yvonne was parachuted with a British-trained French officer into the Lot et Garonne area of south-west France on the night of 18–19 March 1944.

The reception committee proved to be well organized and Lucien and Odette, the respective pseudonyms for the French officer and Yvonne, were quickly removed, pedalling bicycles from the dropping ground to safe houses owned by farmers who co-operated with the Resistance.

On 1 April Yvonne started on a five-day journey to Dole, carrying her cyphers and crystals. They considered it too dangerous for her to take her W/T set as well, so it was agreed that a special courier should send this on to her later.

Safely arrived at Dole, Yvonne and Lucien made their HQ in the flat of the night watchman of the cheese depot, Les Orphelins. This man was Swiss. Both he and his wife helped the SOE pair willingly, and they soon contacted the local Resistance. They met, too, the leader of a Maquis 200 men strong in the Dole, but lacking almost any arms.

As far as a hideout for the W/T transmitter was concerned, the cheese depot seemed to be well placed. German troops constantly called to collect cheese there, no one would have suspected that a place so often visited by the enemy could have been chosen for hiding an instrument so incriminating as a secret wireless transmitter. From the cheese depot, Yvonne worked her transmitter for four months without being detected. This audacious work made it possible to organize during April 1944 five parachute drops totalling 58 containers with arms; five drops in May totalling 72 containers with arms and explosives; and culminating on June 25 with the first-ever attempted mass daylight drop of 423 containers. This last batch contained arms and material for distribution to the growing number of Maquis in the area and it at once raised the morale and aggressiveness of the men.

During the 25 June operation, Yvonne remained on the actual dropping zone with her transmitter for forty-eight hours non-stop, sending frequent crack signals during the night before the operation to keep London informed of the disposition of enemy forces in the vicinity of the proposed drop. Then she assisted in assembling a large convoy of lorries and organizing some 800 men, most of them gendarmes who had joined the Maquis. All were armed and most of them placed in strategic positions to guard against surprise interference from the enemy.

One of the difficulties in this ambitious operation was a German armoured train, located a few miles from the dropping ground and protecting a group of soldiers working on the railway there. But as it happened, the train miraculously moved off the very day on which the operation was scheduled to take place. During the morning of 25 June, Yvonne was even able to get into wireless contact with the approaching three bomber squadrons carrying the expected arms and equipment. Although air raid warnings were sounded in all towns nearby, not a single German came in sight during the whole operation.

All 423 containers floated to earth exactly on schedule, and within an hour they had been loaded on to the lorries with the help of the inhabitants of nearby villages and taken to a forest where Lucion and Yvonne organized their distribution. With the arms and explosives received, good work was achieved in the following weeks, especially putting out of action the Solway chemical works at Tavaux by blowing up and draining the Rhône–Rhine Canal. The telephone exchange and dispatcher at the Dole railway yards were both blown up, and much other damage done.

But before any of this had been accomplished, Lucien and Yvonne started their return journey to Dole on bicycles the morning after the mass drop. Now it was D+20, June 26. Yvonne's wireless transmitter was entrusted to a young member of the Maquis with instructions to bring it by a devious route to the cheese factory. But as fate had it, he was stopped by a German patrol, searched, and the transmitter discovered. After being beaten up, he disclosed under unbearable pressure the location of the headquarters in the cheese depot.

At midday Lucien, Yvonne and several helpers were having lunch there when the Germans surrounded the building. During the drastic search that followed, they found another hidden W/T set. At once they ransacked the whole building, shooting at random through floors and ceilings. Lucien was killed outright. The Swiss night watchman was the only one who succeeded in escaping.

They found Yvonne at 7pm that evening. They hit her in the face, handcuffed her, and took her to the Dijon prison, where she was kept in solitary confinement in a cell. The uncovered sewerage ran through this cell. There they left her without food or water for three days. Then they took her for interrogation by the Gestapo. Throughout this terrible ordeal, Yvonne was handcuffed to the radiator in the room.

Yvonne, the wife of the Swiss night watchman and many other prisoners were all transported in an overcrowded cattle truck with both doors locked to make escape impossible. Their first stop: Saarbrücken. Their second stop: Ravensbrück, the notorious extermination camp. The Germans refused to consider women as prisoners of war. They were subjected to the cruellest treatment – the lot of all political prisoners. Yvonne had to work in the fields. Towards the end of February 1945 she succeeded in being accepted as a menial worker in the infirmary to avoid transportation to another camp to work in a German factory producing war materials. Early in March, she fell so ill that she was admitted as a patient in the infirmary where she had been working. This probably saved her life, for many prisoners were murdered during the last few days before Germany's collapse.

On 25 April a delegate of the Swedish Red Cross arrived at Ravensbrück and within an hour had collected all British inmates in a convoy, which set out for Sweden. After a quarantine of a fortnight, Yvonne was transported to Britain, where she had to be treated in hospital until December before she regained her normal health.

For her outstanding services, Yvonne Baseden was awarded the MBE. She became Mrs Yvonne Bailey and lived in Kenya.

Dublin-born Patricia 'Paddy' O'Sullivan learnt to ride a bicycle in front of a squad of German guards doing their drill. Maureen Patricia O'Sullivan joined the WAAF in the grade of general duties clerk on 7 July 1941. No one would ever have thought that there was anything unusual about ACW O'Sullivan Pers No 450686, but there was. Or there soon would be. Paddy had been educated in France and Belgium, was bilingual in French and spoke Dutch, Flemish and some German. After she had served for some time at the RAF Station at Compton Bassett, near Colne, Wiltshire, where she reached the exalted rank of acting corporal, Paddy decided to do something else.

She applied for the job of sergeant interpreter in the WAAF and also trained as a W/T operator, which stood her in good stead for the mission she eventually undertook. Like all WAAF girls who wanted to join SOE, the first step for Paddy was an intelligence and resource test, to see if she was temperamentally suited for the job. This included such unlikely feminine pursuits as tree climbing, tightrope walking and trials in foxing an enemy. Paddy and another girl were then sent to a lonely island off the coast of Scotland where they learnt to handle mortars, Stens and Tommy guns, worked with demolition parties and went on night exercises. SOE decided that Paddy would make a good W/T operator. Next came the parachute training. Asked if she were nervous, Paddy said: 'Just as much as anyone else. The first, the girl in front of me broke her leg, and another time one of the men refused to jump – which wasn't exactly cheering. However, after the requisite three jumps, I was passed as safe.'

A further course in W/T work completed the preparations and one day she was summoned to SOE headquarters to receive secret orders. Paddy heard how she had to play the part of a Paris doctor's secretary who had been evacuated to the country. She was given her wireless equipment and clothes: two tailored suits especially made in Savile Row with no means of identification on them. For the actual jump she pulled on a camouflage suit.

On the night of 22–23 March 1944 she was to be parachuted into France, near Limoges, with fifteen containers of arms and ammunition. Her reception would be organized by two British officers using Eureka and S-phone apparatus to assist the plane's navigation in finding the dropping ground. Her mission: to act as W/T operator to the Fireman circuit under the command of a British major known as Barthelemy.

The aircraft took off from England at the still of night. Weather conditions were bad and the pilot asked her: 'Would you like to turn back?' He hardly had to point out to Paddy that she would have to jump into a thick fog as well as an occupied country. But soon they were over the target in the heart of pastoral France and Paddy decided literally to take the plunge.

Out into the white night she jumped, floated eerily through the fog, and landed heavily on her back. For a moment she thought she had broken her neck and was dying. Then she passed out. She awoke with breath on her face and felt terribly scared until she realized it was a friendly French *vache*! Then she heard men's voices becoming louder through the gloom. At first she imagined them to be German, but as they grew more distinct she sighed with relief to hear someone swearing profusely in French. The voice next said: 'I think the poor Anglais has broken his neck.'

The reception party obviously had not expected London to send them a girl and when they discovered one there were astonished exclamations. They quickly accepted the surprise, however, and welcomed Paddy warmly, one of them taking the pick and shovel she carried and hurrying to bury the tell-tale parachute, fluttering limply in the fog. The score of Maquis had only two revolvers and two torches between the lot of them, so they eagerly collected the containers bringing them more arms and equipment before hustling Paddy off to a nearby farmhouse for a meal and a rest. She slept for twenty-four hours and then felt fine and ready for anything, which was just as well, for she was to have some hair-raising experiences ahead of her. When she set up her aerial in the utmost secrecy and sent her first message home, she suddenly realized how vital this work was and how careful she must try to be not to fail.

The head of this particular Resistance group, an Englishman posing as French, had organized from scratch a large body of guerrillas, yet he felt dubious of taking the responsibility of hiding a woman. He also considered the job much too tough for a girl. He looked at Paddy's attractive features, her fair hair and blue eyes, and said: 'You'll never pass as a Frenchwoman. You're too blonde.'

'Well, here I am,' Paddy replied, 'and we'll just have to make the best of it.'

And they certainly did. After six weeks, the head received a message from London telling him that there were now two men available if he would like to send Paddy back home. He signalled simply in reply: 'Having trained her I will keep her.'

For the next seven months Paddy's life was fantastic. A single slip would have meant death in any one of a dozen ways. But the French risked their own lives many times by letting her stay in their homes. By moving to a new lodging every few days, she evaded discovery or suspicion.

She made friends with a village schoolmaster and his wife and it seemed quite natural to the Germans that Paddy should be a friend of theirs from Paris who sought hospitality in the country as a change from the starving capital. The schoolmaster passed her on in turn to various other friends and so she became accepted as one of the French community there. The French peasants refused to take more than a nominal sum for her board, although they knew they were shielding a dangerous person. If there were any doubt as to her identity, her equipment would soon have settled it. There was never any means of explaining a wireless transmitter if found.

Paddy's identity card was a perfect forgery, but hidden in the lining of her handbag she had to carry secret codes. Once a German soldier actually took the bag out of her hands and began to examine its contents. It was a terrible moment.

Paddy kept cool. She laughed and joked with the German – distracting him from making a closer scrutiny of the bag. Never having ridden a bicycle, Paddy had no alternative one day but to take her wireless transmitter in a taxi, a procedure forbidden except in extreme emergency. An enemy patrol stopped the taxi but luckily the Germans felt friendly that day and did not try to examine the suitcase, otherwise she would certainly have been caught.

Paddy saw it would be essential in that hilly country around Limoges to learn to ride a bicycle and so was obliged to master the art. Accordingly, right in front of a squad of German guards who were drilling, two of her comrades mounted her on a cycle – and each time she fell off, the Germans roared with laughter. But it was Paddy who was really getting the laugh from them. Later she rode up to fifty kilometres a day.

Under these lighter touches always lurked the reality of the Resistance group and its work, and almost daily came news that one or another member had been captured or shot. No one yet thought of questioning Paddy's presence in the district, so she was able to work quietly on, tapping out her messages, by patience and perseverance becoming a far more efficient operator than when she started. She passed messages asking for vital stores, directives, and containing intelligence on for the waiting ears of SOE.

Radar operators plot and communicate warnings of all approaching enemy aircraft.

WAAF plotters at work in the Operations Room of a fighter station.

Above: Operations Room at Fighter Command HQ. Officers on the dais look down on plotters around the map table. The battle scene changed almost from second to second.

Left: Three gallant WAAFs, all awarded the Military Medal for remaining at their posts under heavy aerial bombardment: Sergeant Joan Mortimer, Corporal Elspeth Henderson and Sergeant Helen Turner.

The Battle of Britain as seen from the ground.

Testing R/T equipment of a Bomber Command Blenheim.

Balloon operators bringing down their charge in 1942.

Radar Operator at Bawdsey
(*Illustrated London News*).

Known by the code-name 'Madeleine', SOE heroine Assistant Section Officer Noor Inayat Khan was executed at Dachau, September 1944.

Joan Pearson, one of the only two WAAF George Cross recipients.

Seven of the seventeen WAAF trained as ferry pilots in Air Transport Auxiliary.

Kathleen Stanley-Smith on the wing of a Hurricane.

All-women ferry pilots' pool at Hamble, Hampshire.

'My first Spitfire
was unbelievable' –
Aimée de Neve.

Serving overseas: three WAAFs in Algiers.

WAAF personnel in VE-Day parade at Ghent.

VJ-Day cheers in Colombo.

During the seven months she spent with the Resistance, she sent 332 W/T messages and despite this heavy traffic also succeeded in training three locally recruited stand-in operators in the special technique needed when using the SOE type of secret transmitters. In the arduous work of coding and decoding, a locally trained English-speaking girl helped her.

Once she was warned to leave her lodging hurriedly and had to take refuge in a barn for forty-eight hours. Rats ran around freely there, and she shivered at the sight of them. It was worse than all her other experiences, she thought.

With the liberation armies advancing, Paddy's job came to an end and she was sent home as a passenger in style. But she was so keen to carry on with her war work that she volunteered for further active service and went through a series of courses with the intention of being used in Germany itself. But by that time it was too late.

After promotion to flight officer, Paddy was awarded the MBE and the Croix de Guerre. On 30 November 1945 she became Mrs Maureen Alvey. That was the happy ending to her particular story.

Muriel Byck and Lilian Rolfe were dropped into France within three nights of each other in April 1944. Neither returned.

Before the war Muriel Tamara Byck had been active as assistant stage manager of the Gate Theatre. During the early years of the war she served in the ARP as a warden, finally enrolling in the WAAF on 12 February 1942. Muriel was selected by SOE in July 1943 and that autumn commenced the usual intensive training, specializing in W/T work. Everyone was impressed with her ability and charm.

Just about the time that Lilian Rolfe was actually being dropped over France, Muriel was briefed for her particular part in the Ventriloquist Resistance circuit in the Loir et Cher district. This was under the command of a Frenchman holding a commission in the British Army. He was known as Antoine. By the date of this briefing, Muriel had heard of her own honorary commission in the WAAF as assistant section officer.

During the night of 8–9 April, she was parachuted with three officers to a reception point near Issoudun. Her papers had been made out in the name of Michelle Bernier and her pseudonym was Violette. Like most other SOE girls, she went about mostly by bicycle, making friends wherever she happened to be. This was considered to be good for giving a convincing background. One day she would transmit from a stately chateau, on another from a garage or a humble isolated farmhouse. It did not matter so long as the occupants were loyal French.

Muriel made her first radio contact with London four weeks after dropping and during May she transmitted for her commanding officer no fewer than twenty-seven messages notifying London of selected parachute dropping grounds, and giving general news of circuit activities and Maquis operations. She also received and deciphered sixteen messages from London and helped to train some locally recruited W/T operators. Then an amazing message was received in London that simply said: 'Violette is dead.'

In view of the urgent strain on wireless communications during the vital phase before and after D-Day, it was not until a month later that the facts could be established back in Britain. At 10am on 23 May Muriel suddenly became unconscious. Petrol was extremely scarce, so it was with the greatest difficulty that her commanding officer managed to get hold of an ambulance to transport her to the hospital in Romorantin. In spite of the efforts of three doctors, all hastily summoned to her, Muriel died of meningitis that same evening at 7pm, without regaining consciousness.

Somehow or other, the Germans learnt of her death, and when the time came they were lying in wait to try and trap any of her associates who might attend her funeral. The French arranged for her body to be placed in the crypt of the Faubourg Saint Roch at Romorantin, to facilitate its removal home by her family after the war. Despite the danger in this Gestapo-infested part of France, her commanding officer considered it his duty to attend the funeral on 25 May. A large number of the local people flocked out of the cemetery, covering her zinc-lined coffin with flowers. Just in time, someone situated at a strategic point told the commanding officer that Gestapo agents were waiting outside the cemetery gates. The officer surreptitiously left the cemetery by climbing over a wall and so avoided arrest. For her courage and service Muriel Byck was recommended for the posthumous award of a mention in despatches.

Lilian Verna Rolfe had an even more tragic end. Together with an American officer, who was to act as arms instructor, Assistant Section Officer Rolfe had been sent to France by Lysander on the night of 5–6 April 1944. They landed in a field located fifteen kilometres southeast of Tours and eleven kilometres southwest of Amboise. Lilian's missions to act as W/T operator to the Historian circuit, under the command of a British officer known as Etienne, operating in the Orleans region.

Through circumstances beyond her control, Lilien was for several weeks separated from Etienne, who was engaged in making contacts to develop his circuit. She finally got in W/T touch with London on his behalf on 2 June and from then on she was in contact almost daily, sending and receiving a large volume of traffic. Her area was honeycombed with Gestapo officials and French militia working with the Germans, so she had to move frequently from place to place to avoid the enemy D/F-ing her set.

Despite the natural nervous strain of this work, Lilian transmitted untiringly and unerringly, her messages always being precise and clear – an important point in secret wireless communications concerning parachute operations, where the slightest ambiguity could have had disastrous effects. Chiefly due to her accurate work, during the invasion month of June, 17 parachute operations took place in her area comprising 397 containers and 134 packages with arms and supplies for the Maquis. By July these operations had been stepped up to 24 parachute drops totalling 520 containers and 178 packages.

On 28 June Etienne was arrested at Olivet. An extremely efficient French officer who had been working in the area for two years took over command of the circuit at once, and Lilian continued her work under his guidance. Early in July, she took part in an engagement between the Maquis and enemy forces near Olivet, but on the last day of that month, Lilian's luck ran out.

The Gestapo raided the house at Nangis where she was spending the night to arrest other people sheltering there. Lilian's bodyguard succeeded in escaping, but Lilian herself was caught. First she was taken to prison in Orleans, later being moved to the Fresnes prison in Paris. The last part of her story came to light only after the war. From inmates of the Ravensbrück concentration camp it was subsequently learnt that Lilian arrived there on 25 August with three other girls. On 5 or 6 September she was sent to Torgau to work in a munitions factory for the Germans. As her health had broken down by that time, she was returned to Ravensbrück on 5 October and, though very ill by then, was transported to Königsberg a fortnight later, where she spent most of her time in the infirmary. On 20 January 1945, Lilian and two other English girls were sent back to Ravensbrück. First they were locked up in the Strafblock and then in the Bunker, from where there was no return. It is believed that Lilian and the other girls were killed there on or about 6 February 1945.

Lilian Rolfe was awarded a posthumous mention in despatches for her courage and devotion to duty.

South African Phyllis Latour was in action in Normandy a month before D-Day. This was a distant cry from her home in the Belgian Congo where she had been brought up by her uncle and aunt. It was in Africa, at the Convent School of St Marie-Jose, Jadoville, that she learned to speak French. In England when war broke out, Phyllis joined the WAAF at the age of twenty. She enlisted as LACW 2041440 as a balloon operator, and received a flight mechanic's training at St Athan, South Wales. But this was not exciting enough and she went into SOE, doing her three parachute jumps without any sign of fear.

Phyllis was commissioned as assistant section officer the same day as Muriel Byck, 1 April 1944, and exactly a month later she was dropped as a W/T operator to the Scientist circuit working in Normandy. Her French papers were made out in the name of Paulette Routal and her pseudonym was Genevieve. The circuit was commanded by a Frenchman holding a British major's commission and known variously as David, Denis and Claude. Two days after her arrival, she succeeded in getting through to London by wireless, but her regular transmissions did not start until June, when she sent the first batch of a total of 135 messages.

This was key country and throughout the month of May Phyllis travelled around the Caen and Vire areas with a British officer, making contacts in preparation for D-Day and after.

Once during their return journey to Champgeneteur they met a German car full of parachutes. Although the German summoned Phyllis and her companion to stop, they managed to separate and make a getaway through a nearby farm. But it was obvious that the enemy now knew of the presence of British parachutists in the region. After destroying compromising documents, they started at two o'clock in the morning to walk to St Mars. After things had quietened down a bit, Phyllis started her regular transmissions from this place. When she was completely installed in her area, Phyllis had no fewer than 17 transmitters at her disposal, located in outlying farms spread over an area of 100 square kilometres in the Mayenne–Calvados area. She actually worked in the midst of the enemy's second line of defence, and owing to their nearness and the activities of their D/F-ing vans, she never transmitted twice running from the same location.

Nevertheless Phyllis was D/F-ed on two occasions. Once when working in the Foret de Pail, her set was detected by a 'vegetable delivery van', the second time by a 'laundry van'. The first time, the German D/F personnel and their 'vegetable van' were destroyed by the local Resistance using hand grenades. The second time, Phyllis stopped transmission due to the timely warning of security watchers.

On yet another occasion while Phyllis was transmitting from St Mars, two German soldiers suddenly entered the house looking for food. With great presence of mind, Phyllis pretended to be packing as she was suffering from scarlet fever – there was an epidemic in the area – and the farmer's daughter lured them away by offering them glasses of cider.

Phyllis Latour was certainly having a hectic life. When her officer's camp was attacked by the Germans one day, Denis sent her on a perilous journey to St Aubin to warn another party and get reinforcements. As if all this were not enough, she also helped in dropping operations, successfully using the S-phone to guide the pilots to the exact spot where the parachutists and containers were to be released.

On D+21 she was recommended for promotion to section officer. At the beginning of August, the advancing Americans liberated their region, but even then the excitement was not quite over. The Allies had to be very careful about screening people, and the Americans had received a faulty description of Phyllis. They kept her for five hours before a guide, who happened to know her, assured them of her proper identity.

On 4 September 1945 Section Officer Phyllis Ada Latour was awarded the MBE and also the Croix de Guerre avec Palme en Bronze. Phyllis returned to the sunshine of Africa in Livingstone, Southern Rhodesia.

While Phyllis was active in Normandy in May 1944, Assistant Section Officer Sonia d'Artois was dropped into France on the 28th – the last WAAF to arrive in France before D-Day. The daughter of a group captain in the RAF, Sonia Esmee Florence Butt joined the WAAF when she was only seventeen. By nineteen she wanted something more adventurous and so offered her services for SOE. She was duly commissioned on the same day as Phyllis, 1 April 1944, and a fortnight later had married Captain Lionel Guy d'Artois of the Canadian army, whom she met on one of the parachute courses she attended.

After her honeymoon and her twentieth birthday, her husband was dropped into France on 23 May, Sonia following five days later. They were not sent to the same district. Sonia, pseudonym Blanche, was sent as courier together with two British officers to the Headmaster circuit in the Le Mans region, commanded by a British officer known as Major Albin. They parachuted safely at La Cropte, eighty kilometres north east of Le Mans, to a reception committee organized by Albin himself, and were taken at once to a safe house. From here Sonia walked eighteen kilometres to the chateau at Brains where she was allowed to rest for three days to get acclimatized before starting her courier and liaison job.

D-Day came and went. On 8 June Major Albin formed two Maquis groups, one in the forest of Charnie, the other at Coulans. Sonja joined the latter, but the hostile attitude of the population near the Coulans forest made it impossible for her to continue training the Maquis in that particular spot. She had to move to the Maquis in Charnie. Here she helped to give arms and explosives instruction and generally assisted the British officer in charge, known as Lieutenant Hugues.

Within a week, Sonia left the Charnie forest with Major Altin for La Mans, where she started liaison work for him with members of his organization dispersed over the whole countryside.

20 June. The Charnie Maquis was attacked by 200 Germans and French militiamen, working with the Germans. Lieutenant Hugues and three Maquis were killed and the rest dispersed, but only after having killed fifteen Germans, including their commanding officer. During this engagement, the Germans captured three cars, one million francs, the W/T set, many arms and parachute material, which enabled them to intercept on the next night two parachute drops of arms and ammunition destined for the Maquis.

Sonia succeeded in guiding two other British officers to another Maquis formed in the forest of Berce. The Germans again came on their tracks, and they got news that all the woods throughout the department were about to be searched.

The disaster suffered by the Charnie Maquis and the interruption of W/T contact with London prompted a change of tactics. The men split into six small groups located in various parts of the region around Le Mans. Sonia had the job of courier and liaison officer between these dispersed groups. Things went better after that.

On 28 August Sonia went to Loch in accordance with a message received to contact Major Antoine, the leader of the powerful Ventriloquist circuit. She arranged with him for London to be informed of the location of dropping grounds selected in the Headmaster circuit area for delivering a new W/T set and also arms.

Soon after her return to La Mans the advancing Americans liberated the town. Sonia then helped Major Albin organize intelligence missions behind the German lines and she took part herself in several which brought back vital information on enemy dispositions to the US 5th Armored Division. Returning from one of these three-day missions by car, Albin and Sonia suddenly came under fire while approaching a bridge over that part of the Seine. They expected to find Americans there, but saw instead that German SS was guarding the bridge. They quickly abandoned their car and made for the fields in a frantic effort to reach some smaller road, but to their dismay they found this also to be guarded by German sentries. They were arrested and kept for interrogation for four hours. Fortunately, however, the Germans believed their plausible cover story and later let them proceed to Bar sur Seine, about a mile away. On arrival there, they found the town occupied by the enemy and completely pillaged. Almost all the population was hiding in cellars. During the evening, the Germans took Major Altin away as a hostage, and Sonia was sent to fetch his coat, not being detained herself.

She met a Frenchman on the way who asked her to tell his fiancée where he was. Sonia agreed to do so if she could spend the night at this girl's home. The man directed here there, but on the way she was attacked by a couple of German soldiers, one of them drunk. She was still carrying compromising documents, but she managed to cope with the two men.

Major Altin calmly managed to escape next day and rejoin her, and together they walked towards the American lines, which they reached two days later. Sonia's mission was at an end. Despite her youth, Sonia d'Artois earned the respect and admiration of all the men in the Maquis for her gallantry. Her commanding officer described her as 'absolutely fearless'. On 4 September 1945 she was awarded the MBE, the same decoration as Phyllis Latour and Paddy O'Sullivan, and on the same day.

Christine Granville could be called the first and the last of all the WAAF officers in SOE – and certainly one of the greatest. She started secret work almost as soon as war broke out, but it was only during the later years that she held an honorary commission as flight officer in the WAAF.

Born in 1915 of a proud Polish family, Christine was twenty-seven, widowed and living in East Africa in the summer of 1939. As soon as she heard that Hitler had invaded her country, she sailed on the first available ship for England, arriving in October. Her maiden name was Countess Skartek; her married name Countess Gizycka; and her nom de guerre Christine Granville. It was under the last name that she won fame.

Soon after her arrival in England, Christine was approached with the proposal that she should return to her native country in order to organize groups of underground resistance, the infiltration of propaganda material, and any other activities designed to keep up the spirit of resistance of the overpowered Poles. Christine Granville set out almost at once for Hungary, where she established her base for future operations.

Being an expert skier and knowing the mountains around Zakopane intimately, she had soon opened a route via Czechoslovakia into Poland. Before she had to leave Hungary finally, she had crossed the Polish border six times and the Slovakian border eight times, on foot and on skis.

In the course of her work into Poland from Hungary, Christine was instrumental in getting the first escaped British prisoners of war returned home, and also for the organization of one of the most efficient routes in central Europe for the escape of Allied nationals generally. It was via this route that hundreds of Poles and other Allied civilian internees were brought safely out to Allied territory. Many of these would doubtless have died if they had not got away.

Apart from these activities – more than enough for most people – Christine was busy collecting military and political information on Poland and Hungary, and in carrying out sabotage of communications on the main Danube route leading into Germany from Yugoslavia, Rumania and Hungary. Not surprisingly really, Christine was arrested twice during this time, once in Slovakia and the second time in Hungary. On each occasion she managed to escape. Unfortunately, the second time she was caught, in 1941 in Budapest, she lost all her identity papers, which made life more difficult for her.

In spite of this, Christine succeeded in May of that year in escaping from Hungary to Yugoslavia, where she worked for a while for the British. These were still comparatively early days in the wartime career of this fantastic woman. Making her way through Bulgaria, she reached Turkey. In Istanbul she helped the SOE Polish section in their courier and contact work until she was called to Cairo some time in the autumn of 1941 to carry out similar work in the Middle East and more specifically in Syria, where she proved particularly useful during the Syrian campaign.

So Christine had worked under the nose of the Nazis in countries as far apart as her beloved Poland, Czechoslovakia, Hungary, Yugoslavia, possibly Romania, Turkey, Egypt and now Syria. She stayed in the Middle East for a long time after that on secret duties. While she was out there, she underwent W/T training and a special parachute jumping course, so becoming the first woman to be so trained by SOE in the Middle East.

June 1944 and D-Day in Normandy meant more preparation on the Mediterranean fronts. Christine was transferred to North Africa where the SOE Algiers mission wanted her experienced services. Soon after, the Allies would be invading southern France and Special Operations Executive had to pave the path for them. On 7 July Christine was parachuted to the Vercors, in south France, under the codename of Pauline. She hit the ground so hard that the impact broke the butt of the revolver she had in her pocket, but she did not suffer any serious hurt and brushed this aside lightly.

She had a whole series of shocks in the months that followed. Her job was to plan every means possible of causing chaos to the enemy when the Allies should eventually land on the Riviera coast. Those three months of July to September, she worked mainly in the area east of the River Rhône, constantly travelling through enemy country as assistant to the senior British officer organizing resistance in that region.

Towards the end of July, Christine found herself on the Vercors Plateau, which was defended by 2,000 lightly armed Maquis. Here she stayed throughout the greater part of the famous attack launched against them by the Germans with forces including airborne troops and an armoured division. Christine somehow managed to escape through the lines on the day the Vercors Plateau fell to the enemy.

At the end of July, Christine made a twenty-four-hour trip on foot over dangerous mountain paths into Italy, where she contacted the only partisan group in the Italian Alps capable of being useful to the Allied cause. This group numbered two thousand strong, under the leadership of Marcelini, and held the heights between the two roads leading into France at Briancon. Christine realized at once the possibilities of Marcelini as a leader. While she was with them, they were suddenly attacked by a force of over 5,000 Germans, hunting them out in the mountains. Christine did all she could to help and finally put Marcelini and all those left of his band in touch with the British Resistance organizer whose mission was to contact Italians all along the French frontier.

Christine accomplished this mission at great personal risk, as she had to pass through the German lines under fire to get both there and back. It was on her return route that one of her two narrowest escapes of this phase occurred. She encountered a Nazi patrol almost head-on. Thinking instantly, she hurled hand grenades at them, and escaped unscathed to round off her job with a report to her commanding officer.

Her other close call came about this time, too, when she met an enemy night patrol complete with tracker dog. Christine did not want a showdown at this place and time, so she hid in a potato field. The dog discovered her lurking there under the vegetation, but instead of barking and betraying her, it responded to a whispered call from her and stayed nestling near her until the enemy gave up looking for it!

The little village of Seyne in the Basse Alpes was then the main base of Roger, or Colonel Francis Cammaerts, Christine's commanding officer. Two more officers arrived at Seyne about this time, one British, Xan Fielding, the other French, Major Chasuble.

Fielding remembered Christine's nervous gestures, breathless manner of speech and glamorous figure, but she camouflaged this in an austere blouse and skirt which, with her short, carelessly combed dark hair and complete absence of make-up on her delicately featured face, gave her the appearance of an athletic art student.

Then, as so often occurred in work of this kind, came a brutal blow. On 13 August, Cammaerts, Fielding and Chasuble were all arrested in Digne. This represented a serious setback to resistance operations in the whole area, particularly as it happened only two days before the Allied landing in the south of France. Christine was immediately informed. She endeavoured to find out the strength of the guard on her colleagues, and at first tried to organize a 'cutting out' raid by the local French patriots. It turned out to be impossible to collect a force large enough for this plan, however, which had to be abandoned. There was then very little time left to try and rescue the officers, who were due to be shot on 17 August at 9pm.

In a supreme effort to bring off the apparently impossible, Christine made a heroic decision. She presented herself to two of the Gestapo officials. She had two interviews with them, aware that they knew full well she was a British agent. She was risking torture and her life for her friends. Then the impossible happened. Luckily the Allied landings had come just in time, on 15 August. Christine told them that she knew the Allied armies were a mere thirty miles away and that Digne was surrounded. This was quite untrue.

By an amazing mixture of bravado and bluff, she worked upon their fears so much that they were forced to wonder what their ultimate fate might be if they went ahead with their intentions. Christine went on quickly to tell them that if they were to render the Allies the service of releasing their three important prisoners, their own position would be changed for the better. She even said she was in a position to keep her word, as her uncle was General Montgomery! At last the force of her character prevailed, after an anxious wait of an hour following the final interview. The officers were expecting to be shot at any time, but instead they were driven to the outskirts of the town with the French 'milicien' responsible for their arrest. The car stopped at a lonely point and there they saw the figure of Christine, silhouetted against a white wall. She squeezed into the front seat.

At the edge of a steep embankment, the car stopped once more. The milicien jumped out, buried his discarded garments and got in again. Then they drove off in the direction of the mountains. They had given the milicien safe conduct. They were free. Christine had done it.

Later in August, Christine had a task after her own heart. She made contact with the Polish elements in the German occupation forces and, speaking their own language, she succeeded in convincing seventy of them to desert the Germans. Bringing their arms with them, these men crossed the Col de Larche and joined the Resistance fighters.

The following month the area where Christine was working was overrun by the advancing Allied forces, and on 5 October she reported to the resistance headquarters then created in Avignon. Her mission over, she returned to England in November.

On her return, Christine was still keen for further work in the field, volunteering to join a party of British officers to be parachuted into Poland. She was accepted for this task and went to Italy to await infiltration. But Poland was overrun by the Russians before the party could go in, so she returned to Cairo until she was finally demobilized. For her superb services to the Crown, Christine was awarded British naturalization in January 1947, while her honours included the George Medal, the OBE and the Croix de Guerre.

But that was not the end of the story. In 1952, Christine was stabbed to death in a London hotel by Dennis Muldowney, an ex colleague whose advances she had rejected.

Chapter 7

The WAAF at Home

After the Munich crisis in the autumn of 1938, RAF companies were formed in the new women's army force, the Auxiliary Territorial Service. The plan did not work out well, however, and it was decided in May 1939 to create a separate women's service for the RAF, to be christened the WAAF, the Women's Auxiliary Air Force. This became finally effective from 28 June 1939, and the new WAAF uniform was procured just in time for its first appearance at the Royal Review of the Services and Civil Defence Organisations in Hyde Park on 2 July. On 28 August the Air Ministry authorized enrolment of recruits as telephonists, teleprinter operators, cooks, plotters and mess staff, and the calling up of personnel required for duty where their company was affiliated, so most of the existing officers and airwomen were already mobilized when war broke out.

A noticeable feature among recruits was the high proportion who showed some degree of foot deformity, ascribed mainly to badly made or ill-fitting shoes. These girls were usually accepted and given treatment from qualified chiropodists, one of the trades in which WAAF were later enrolled. Despite these and such other headaches as VD, which reached its peak rate of 3.5 per 1,000 in 1942, the health of the WAAF was generally very good. Credit for this could be given partly to the living conditions, despite the fact that the sleeping areas for officers, sergeants and aircraftwomen varied to the extent of 140, 70 and 45 square feet of floor respectively!

Then there were the recurring problems resulting from the failure of the official mind to grasp that they were dealing with women, not men. The works department, for instance, could see no reason for connecting the ablutions hut to the sleeping huts. Since airmen were expected to proceed in the open air from their hut to the wash place, why should not the WAAF do likewise? The discomfort of such cold journeys and the impropriety of making women walk about in a state of deshabille became matters more serious to the WAAF than Whitehall could comprehend.

Uniform was a headache for a long time. When war was declared, supplies were not available for even one tenth of the pre-war WAAF. Every effort to hurry up manufacture included inviting demands for raincoats, brassards, skirts, collars, tie, shoes, berets, stockings, overalls and underwear. In November 1939, fleecy linings, blue slacks, gloves and cardigan were added, but many weeks passed before the girls were kitted to even this meagre scale. For the first few months of the war, airwomen were seen about in a strange array of civilian clothing, varied with an occasional issue garment. Larger consignments of tunics and skirts arrived in February 1940 and by April most of the WAAF had one complete outfit.

Early in 1940 it became apparent that a raincoat even with a fleecy lining would not give the girls enough protection throughout the wartime winters, when they were often in exposed conditions such as airfield sites. The Treasury forced the withdrawal of the raincoat altogether, rather than authorize two outdoor coats, and so for the rest of the war airwomen had to step out in the rain wearing either their greatcoats – an awkward garment to dry – or an unwieldy groundsheet, which dripped rain into her shoes, and was not always so funny as it sounds. The initial issue of greatcoats came on 2 October 1940, with the war a year old and the Battle of Britain won. This was a measure of the country's lack of preparation for full-scale war.

The 'suit, working, serge', or battle blouse and trousers, was designed for the WAAF balloon operator when she first appeared in 1941. From that moment, practically every other trade presented a strong case for entitlement to wear these suits. They caught on with the speed of feminine fashion in peacetime, and soon everyone was wearing trousers, until, as with all fashions, airwomen swung the other way in 1945 and once more they were to be seen in blouses and skirts, not trousers.

In the earlier days, a lot of uncertainty prevailed over the right scale of equipment for the girls' quarters. A bleak scale, parallel to the men's standards, existed throughout the war, and in actual fact most airwomen had in their sleeping quarters only a bed (after 1943 quite often a double bunk) and bedding, two feet of shelving with two hooks, half a small mat and quarter of a folding chair. This resembled the ATS scale, but was below the WRNS standard, and far lower than Canadian and American service women's conditions in Britain.

Actual working conditions were laid down in 1940, but the pressure of the war made adherence to them impossible. The rules were that WAAFs should work eight hours a day, forty-eight hours a week, having one day off a week, and have meals every four hours, except during sleep. But the shortage of manpower and labour generally became too acute and the girls worked nearer the RAF's level of sixty hours a week than the stipulated figure. The cooks suffered perhaps more than any other trade from the rapid expansion of the RAF and WAAF. For most of the war they worked under trying conditions in kitchens, having to feed far more than the number for which they had been built. Despite all the difficulties, the cooks remained among the most cheerful and willing of all WAAFs, accepting the long hours and lack of glamour with good heart. This is a tribute to them all.

The recruiting staff of the WAAF were subjected to bombing in the big cities and their behaviour came up to the standard set on operational stations of the RAF. At Bristol, the area headquarters and the hostel in which the airwomen lived were both hit and three girls were killed; Birmingham area headquarters received a direct hit, too; and several combined recruiting centres in the south were severely damaged. Despite the Blitz, the London and south eastern area headquarters never failed to send off the daily draft of recruits to the appropriate centre, although the staff and recruits sometimes had to spend half the day in the shelters, and railway stations were often not functioning.

For the record, here is the total number of recruits accepted annually during the years 1939 to 1945:

Period	Volunteers	NSA	Total
Sept 1939–Dec 1940	14,546		14,546
Jan 1941–Dec 1941	81,928		81,928
Jan 1942–Dec 1942	62,091	16,246	78,337
Jan 1943–Dec 1943	11,144	17,192	28,336
Jan 1944–Sept 1944	11,225	494	11,719
July 1945–Dec 1945	2,383		2,383
Total	183,317	33,932	217,249

The next table shows where all these girls were trained at WAAF recruit depots:

Location	Date opened	Date closed
West Drayton	30 Oct 1939	17 Sept 1940
Harrogate	18 Sept 1940	30 May 1941
Innsworth	30 Dec 1940	15 Aug 1943
Bridgnorth	30 May 1941	30 Sept 1942
Morecambe	1 Oct 1941	25 Feb 1943
Wilmslow	25 Feb 1943	–

The RAF station at West Drayton became the first recruit depot from necessity rather than choice eight weeks after the war started. Planned as a transit camp, it provided virtually only sleeping and messing accommodation. The recreational facilities were meagre, the surroundings sordid, low-lying and liable to fog and flood. Apart from that it was ideal! Fortunately the peak period of intake occurred during the early summer of 1940, when most of the training could be done outdoors.

The staff consisted mainly of WAAF personnel, and considering all the obstacles and their own inexperience, they achieved quite remarkable results. If they had not been sincere and conscientious, the West Drayton episode might have been a debacle, something that could not be afforded at this stage of the war.

During 1940, the intake of recruits gradually increased until the depot's capacity became exceeded. By then, too, continuous air raids were making training almost impossible, since the recruits spent most of each night in the trenches and most of each day making hurried dashes to the shelters. Added to that, the RAF wanted West Drayton for radar training, so a new home had to be found for the WAAF anyway.

In spite of a general wish to house the WAAF depot on an RAF station, on 18 September 1940 it moved to a number of hotels and schools in the healthy town of Harrogate. Thereafter, the WAAF depots crossed and recrossed the map of England, as the table has indicated. The depots in their wanderings experienced most types of home.

From the training point of view, a hutted camp on the lines of Bridgnorth or Wilmslow proved the most satisfactory, since at a depot like this airwomen got a good idea of the life they might expect at their stations. Moreover, it became clear that a training depot needed a permanent location, as only in such surroundings could a school nature and the instructors give proper attention to their trainees.

But the ideal was not always attainable during the war, and pressure of events often forced the WAAF to accept less than the desirable. In August 1941, at a time of rapidly rising substitution of women for men, it was assumed that the weekly intake would be raised from 2,000 to 3,000 a week, and later to 4,000. To keep pace with these demands, No 3 Depot was opened at Morecambe on 1 October 1941, and the No 2 Depot at Innsworth converted into a receiving centre only, to take 2,700 recruits who were enrolled, kitted and then sent to Morecambe for their basic training. This arrangement enabled the 4,000-a-week figure to be handled, but it could not be regarded as ideal. The recruit had a few bewildering days at Innsworth before leaving the hut and station life she was beginning to get used to, and then taking a long trip to a depot of a very different kind.

Innsworth was a camp of the normal RAF pattern, but Morecambe was a north-west seaside town where the girls had to billeted on the landlady of some local boarding house, and lived a hybrid existence, which seemed to be neither airwoman nor civilian. Their billets were scattered all over the town, and both training and discipline consequently proved difficult. Recruits had to be marched through the streets to cinemas and halls for lectures, and drill on the parade by the sea in the eyes of the public.

Eventually came the move from Morecambe to Wilmslow, where the hutted camp conception returned. In contrast to the varied history of recruit depots geographically, the actual training showed little change throughout the war, and in this first fourteen-day course, the girls went through the medical, enrolment and kitting routine and received the following training: organization and administration (including four lectures on hygiene), fourteen hours; anti-gas and station defence. fifteen hours; drill, twelve hours; and physical training, six hours. After basic training, of course, came trade training and later on NCOs' courses for those progressing.

After the introduction of cadet training into the RAF, a similar scheme was considered for the WAAF. On 12 February 1942, it was agreed that the initial course at the WAAF Officers' School should be converted into an officer's cadet training course. The hasty and large-scale commissioning of WAAF officers during 1941, the time of great expansion, had presented a problem in the form of a number of mature and unsuitable officers. The main reason, therefore, for converting the first course to an Officer Cadet Training Unit (OCTU) was to give a more thorough training to the women who were to become officers. And commissions would not henceforth be granted until the cadets had completed their course satisfactorily.

The first cadets actually arrived in August 1942, the date by the way of the Markham Report on the WAAF, which recommended such an OCTU and so was outdated even as it appeared. To show their state of transition between airwomen and officer, the cadets wore white bands around their caps. They were still paid as airwomen but lived under officers' mess conditions, which they shared with their instructors. As a contribution towards mess maintenance, they were required to pay the sum of sixpence a day.

During the first few months, all cadets shared the same syllabus. Its keynote was the changed status of the cadets. Instead of looking for orders they were learning to give them. The course consisted of drill, anti-gas training, physical training, general service knowledge, RAF organization and administration, WAAF administration and welfare, and Air Force law applied to the WAAF. It must be admitted that in those first months of the OCTU, the high rate of failures caused alarm and despondency at the Air Ministry.

In December the WAAF officers' school moved from Loughborough to Windermere, and the OCTU went with it, a revised system of training being introduced, involving a longer course. When the Officers' School moved on to Stratford in July 1944, the OCTU remained at Windermere, in pleasanter and more spacious accommodation of the Belsfield and Old England Hotels. Conditions could scarcely have been better, nor surroundings more idyllic, though the damp and enervating climate was not conducive to concentrated study. Despite this, the girls had to work from 8.30am to 6.00pm six days a week.

The training of WAAF officers, as distinct from the cadet scheme, had a chequered career. During late 1939 and early 1940, a small number of officers were admitted to the junior course in admin at the RAF School then at Gerrards Cross. These students did very well, but the arrangement lasted only a short time. The initial service training for the newly appointed officers began, followed soon after by the beginning of the training courses for junior officers – but by a combination of circumstances, the senior WAAF officers throughout the war received virtually no training at all!

A large number of code and cypher officers were appointed during that first winter of the war, and to give them at least a smattering of general service information, a course of five and a half days was planned, to be held at Reading. This proved inadequate in every way, as the training had to be in the hands of WAAF officers who themselves had only a sketchy background of knowledge.

By December 1940, better accommodation was found for the

code and cypher course, which moved to Bulstrode Park, Gerrards Cross, where WAAF officer training really began to blossom. A new unit was formed, named the WAAF Officers' School, under a WAAF commanding officer. A country house in large grounds, Bulstrode Park made an apt setting for the school, with good accommodation and its proximity to London for visiting lecturers.

Henceforth this code and cypher course became the initial one for all new WAAF officers, while for the benefit of many officers commissioned earlier in 1940, an administrative course was also introduced. Soon after this, though, the capacity of Bulstrode began to become outstripped and the officers' courses moved to Loughborough Technical College, with its capacity of 350 as against 100 at Bulstrode. The first intakes were on 26 July 1941.

Within a year, however, Loughborough was wanted for other purposes, so an alternative had to be found. The OCTU was started, split between Grange-over-Sands and Loughborough, and then in September 1942 Windermere had been selected as suitable for the WAAF Officers' School. It was here that the training took on a more human note, and an instructors' course was projected as well. Voice production and speech training were tackled, with the aim of training officers in the technique of lecturing. Windermere went a long way to changing the unbending atmosphere of former days, and the WAAF administration learned and taught much of value while there.

The last wartime move of the Officers' School was to Stratford-upon-Avon, the best of all its homes. Conditions here were very civilized to the extent of many single rooms, all with fitted washbasins, while there was good lecture room accommodation under one roof, and other facilities. The only real snag lay in the lack of a parade ground, which meant drill and parades taking place in front of the Shakespeare Memorial Theatre and public gardens, thus attracting the embarrassing interest of the many visitors to the town. What would the Bard have thought of the WAAF parading in the heart of his home town?

So much for the initial training of airwomen and officers, but what did they do after that? The answer really stems from the reason for the creation of the WAAF – substitution of men by women in the Royal Air Force. It was originally intended that the WAAF should not grow very large. The establishment in peacetime was about 3,000, and the strength some 2,000. But when substitution began, recruitment up to 10,000 and then 20,000 was agreed. Compared with the numbers finally achieved, these figures seem very small. The WAAF reached the remarkable maximum strength of 181,835 at one point: more than the whole strength of the RAF at the outbreak of war.

By May 1940 it was officially recognized that it was unfortunate that so small a proportion of WAAF trades had a direct relation to aircraft, so methods of employing girls on duties directly connected with repairs and maintenance were examined. By the end of the year, WAAF officers were replacing RAF officers on code and cypher and on photographic work, and the employment of airwomen had spread to the following trades: instrument mechanic, wireless telegraphy (slip reader) operator, fabric worker (balloon), fabric worker (balloon rigger), equipment assistant, clerk special duties, clerk general duties, clerk accounts, administrative, teleprinter operator, radio operator, cook, telephone operator, mess and kitchen staff, motor transport driver, dental surgery attendant, sick quarters attendant, aircraft hand.

By the end of the year, women had been substituted in fifteen officer appointments and fifty-nine airmen's trades, in addition to seventeen ancillary trades established solely for WAAF and four specialist WAAF trades. When substitution was first mooted, it had been assumed that in all trades three women would be needed to replace two men, but experience showed that it could be carried out on the basis of one woman for one man, generally speaking. Presumably the original three-to-two was a male idea! The equality achieved was very gratifying for the girls.

Because of the belief that women were not mechanically minded and so unable to undertake very skilled work, substitution in the technical trades came slowly. Certain of the skilled trades were broken down, the simpler part of the work being converted into a purely WAAF concern, such as sparking plug tester, charging board operator and instrument mechanic. But in 1943 these trades were declared obsolete, as the girls had proved themselves fully able to do all the duties of the 'parent' trades – flight mechanic, electrician II and instrument repairer II.

For some time, these and other comparable technical trades were referred to as experimental, but it had to be conceded finally that the experiment was highly successful and a substitution up to fifty per cent of personnel was authorized. In October 1943 official recommendation said that substitution as flight mechanics (air frame) and (engine) should be confined to non-operational units, but this edict was not always heeded, as the Air Ministry itself admits. The only way in which women could not cope with one-for-one duty was where the work proved actually too tiring and then the girls could not be expected to do as long a day as a man.

The signals branch expanded enormously as soon as war started, and telephone and teleprinter operators were among the first WAAF to take the place of men. Throughout the war, in these trades they formed three-quarters of the strength, and the girls did one-for-one duty successfully, as the awards during the Battle of Britain have already shown.

More caution was exercised in the other signals trades. The exception was radiotelephone operator, though in this case there was reluctance due to the nature of the language passing through (not bad language, but the technical terms normally used!). The women weathered this, however, and fifty per cent substitution was the order. Some girls undertook wireless operator duties, their work being largely concerned with interception of signals, involving knowledge of foreign languages. Their success at this paved the path for more general W/T work later.

Despite early doubts too, the WAAF took over as wireless mechanics and radar mechanics, though the numbers were not large. The choice of women in many of the signals trades such as these was also limited by the undesirability of using WAAFs at dispersal points, or detached or isolated units. The rule that WAAFs should not be on night duty alone made a further limitation, though the rules were ignored on occasion. Much of the signals work involved repetitious duty, but the girls bore it brightly, adapting themselves both to slack and stress equally well.

The same conclusions applied generally to officers in the signals branches. Code and cypher officers began by filling home posts, but later went to many overseas theatres. Few people would disagree that women were on the whole more successful than men at this work. They seemed to appreciate the importance of combining accuracy with speed. By October 1943 it had been decided that even the senior posts at commands could be filled by WAAFs.

One achievement deserves special mention. In April 1942, WAAF officers were asked to be responsible for the code and cypher work of the War Cabinet. This meant not only the codes and cyphers, but all the clerical work connected with the reproduction and circulation of signals to and from Chiefs of Staff, War Cabinet and Prime Minister. The same few officers were entrusted with the work from start to finish, chosen of course for their technical ability and discretion. The Air Ministry Special Signals Office, later renamed the Cabinet Offices Cypher Office, was set up in the Air Ministry, Whitehall, and officers worked directly with the Defence Office.

From the time of the vital Malta convoys and the assault on Madagascar, all through the planning of the North African landings and the assault on the coast of Western Europe to the eventual surrender of Germany, the atom bomb and the surrender of Japan, most of the signals between the War Cabinet and the commanders in the field and the Chiefs of Staff Mission in America passed through the WAAFs' hands.

When Winston Churchill left the country to confer with other heads of state, the signal traffic became almost too heavy to be borne. When he went to Marrakesh in December 1943, and again nine months later to Quebec, some of the officers went with him to handle the signals. Five WAAF officers were present at Yalta, four to help distribute the signals in the Defence Office and one to advise the WRNS whom on this occasion did the actual cypher work. Three WAAF officers attended the Potsdam conference as well.

It was in 1940 that the Air Council investigated replacing RAF barrage balloon operators by airwomen. Due to the nature of the work this was the most extravagant form of replacement in the service. The ratio at first was 20:9, then 16:9 and finally 14:9.

It was not the girls' fault, of course, that they needed one and a half women to each man. It was just a physical fact. With the girls, came the call for more accommodation, the WAAFs having two huts and an ablution hut whereas the men had only one hut altogether. Extra men at flight and squadron headquarters were needed to lift the folded balloons on and off the trucks and to help the WAAFs in handling the balloon in high winds or bad weather. The WAAFs had to have more mechanical aids in the actual balloon handling gear, and the preparation of the balloon bed, and more aids to start up the engines of the winches. But again, none of this was their fault.

The WAAF balloon operators were a happy lot, liking their work and their life on the site. There was little trouble, surprising considering that they were mostly very young, in small groups with young NCOs in charge, and often in or near dock areas or on lonely sites. The balloon girls served with great gallantry, but despite this, replacing men was not a complete success. WAAFs could not be sent overseas or man mobile balloons. When a curtain of balloons was wanted to protect London from the flying bombs, Balloon Command was hard put to find enough RAF crews to man them. The girls could not help, because there were no concrete balloon beds, no central anchorage, no living or cooking accommodation and they just could not cope with the heavy lifting necessary under these conditions. But because of the very hardships and obstacles, the record of the WAAFs on balloons is perhaps as outstanding as any in the war.

Another all-weather WAAF branch was motor transport driver, one of the few pre-war trades. Girls who became drivers could rarely be persuaded to change their job for other or more responsible work. Conditions were far from ideal, and there was a lot of blackout driving, which cannot be imagined unless experienced. Finding a bed and a meal were other problems for these girls. At first, women were allowed to drive vehicle only up to fifteen cwts, but this figure later doubled to thirty cwts. They were not allowed to lift heavy weights, however, change heavy wheels or crank up engines from cold. On the whole, girls did not do duty at radar stations except in southern England, as more northern stations were considered unsuitable because of the possibility of breakdown in isolated parts of the country. These limitations apart, the WAAFs drove far, wide and long.

Still associated with the open air, some WAAFs served as meteorological assistants working long hours on observation in all weathers and at odd hours of the day and night. A certain standard of education was a prerequisite for this job, but the girls who did it found that it bore a close relationship to flying operations and so considered it worthwhile. There were even some WAAF officers with a university or similar degree. These officers served as weather forecasters at selected places, such as night fighter sector control stations, as it was thought that they could not be used on briefing aircrew on weather. This naturally remained one of the smaller branches of the service.

One of the biggest branches was that involving the clerical trades – one of the least glamorous, though most useful. Girls quickly took over airmen's jobs in offices, with the usual accomplishments of shorthand and typing plus an ability to pick up the necessary routine. They were also more efficient than the men! By VE-Day, WAAFs were filling some 43 per cent of the total clerical posts in the RAF. In April 1942, it was decided that women could work in the RAF post offices, including handling mailbags. Experience showed subsequently that the girls got more adept on these postal duties than their counterparts, though there were some restrictions on handling mailbags above 50lbs in weight, requiring male brute force.

Accounting clerks proved to be another outlet for the WAAFs, and while the women served in great numbers, there were far fewer accounts branch WAAF officers.

Personnel selection clerks were entirely WAAF in the latter part of the war. These officers and airwomen had responsibility for administering the psychological and educational tests and handling the follow-up data. The efficiency of the WAAFs in this trade assured the success of such varied aspects as aircrew grading and classification, instructor selection, vocational advice service and normal ground staff selection.

Various kinds of officer posts became gathered under the heading of Administration G. The earliest of these were for assistant adjutants. WAAFs could undertake these duties, it was decided, though as the WAAF were not part of His Majesty's Forces, they had no power to give orders to the RAF. Some WAAF officers did in fact graduate to adjutants proper, though they could not sit on courts martial.

Equipment assistants did all that was wanted of them, with the provision that they did not try to shift heavy stores. Officers were also commissioned in this sphere, but civilian foremen and labourers often objected to being controlled by women, many of whom were far younger than them! The war effort took second place to the eternal struggle between the sexes. On 1 July 1943 there were no fewer than 280 WAAF equipment officers.

Another routine branch was that embracing the domestic trades: mess stewards, cook, waitress, batwoman, aircrafthand (general duties). Airwomen did not perform mess steward duties until 1941, when the shortage of stewards became serious. There was discussion for some time as to whether a clerk or a cook was really the best type of person for this trade, and selection seemed to be getting difficult.

In the early days of catering, WAAF cooks were used in WAAF messes only, but 1940 saw the start of service training for cooks, and during that year they began to replace men in RAF kitchens. But by then, reports were coming in of cooks having to work too long hours and getting insufficient time off. Sickness seemed to be much more prevalent among cooks than other trades. So an energetic recruiting drive was launched with better conditions, including cloakrooms and restrooms. There is nothing much more that can be said about the WAAF cooks except to praise their years of hard behind-the-scenes life. The same applies to WAAF waitresses, introduced into service messes rather to replace civilians than airmen.

The last trade among airwomen in domestic duties was WAAF aircraft hand. She had to do mainly rough work in the messes, and most WAAF officers felt that the employment of women aircraft hands in service messes and kitchens was undesirable and could only be tolerated under the stress of war.

Early in 1942, a dozen officers were tried out on catering. They were all assistant section officers, with good records and civilian domestic science qualifications. They had a tough time proving to their male opposite numbers in the RAF that this could be a branch for girls, but the 12 guinea pigs did become the forerunners of 252 WAAF catering officers in the service on 1 July 1943.

Lastly to the more specialized trades. The first WAAFs to be used in operations rooms were the special duties clerks or plotters. They had the privilege of being among the first women to be trained in the service, and took up their stations in ops rooms soon after war began. Known as watchkeepers, like Audrey Smith they proved a striking success and their strength ran into several thousands. On 1 September 1942 there were 6,228; on 1 July 1943, 7,395. This amounted to about half of the RAF strength. Wherever aircraft flew, there were plotters needed to represent the overall picture of operations in Fighter Command, Bomber Command, Coastal Command. A typical operations room board used by Coastal Command measured thirty feet square fixed vertically to the wall. The WAAFs who marked the latest positions of planes were harnessed like marionettes or trapeze artistes. They went up a steep ladder and then simply stepped off, with their harness like that of a parachute attached to a lone wire working friction pulleys. These girls literally walked on air as they marked on the wall map the minute-to-minute information for the benefit of RN and RAF officers safely standing on the floor.

It was April 1941 before the Air Ministry considered using WAAF officers in ops rooms, and in June of that year Bomber Command proposed to replace RAF officers by WAAFs in certain operations and intelligence posts. From a psychological viewpoint, they did not think it advisable for girls to interrogate aircrews, though in later times the WAAF officers frequently did so.

Other officer posts were those of filterer, air raid warning liaison and movement control liaison. Coastal Command asked for officers as assistant controllers in ops rooms – half the posts for flying officers being allotted to women. By 1 July 1943, the highest strength date of the WAAF, 327 intelligence officers were serving, 193 in ops rooms and 108 filter and filterer officers.

The trade of medical orderly was introduced into the WAAF forty-eight hours before the war opened. They were meant to be used for nursing airwomen sick in billets, hostels or WAAF sick quarters. Moreover, they were to be women of 'the motherly type' and over thirty-five years old. But it was hard to find women of this sort with the right experience, and in the early days the sad fact emerged that women with no aptitude for anything else tended to be mustered as medical orderlies.

The lower age limit of 35 was most inept, as it ruled out all girls who had done perhaps part of a hospital training course and would have been good potential material. Many motherly types also proved to be quite unteachable, too! Complaints soon started to reach the medical training establishment and depot about the unsuitability of many of these well-meaning women, and so it was decided to assess and train them all. In August, the trade group M was formed and the lower age reduced to 25, while anyone with experience could be accepted at 18. Nursing orderlies became the new category and a new chapter opened. After 1942, a few nursing orderlies were specially trained in burns work. The duties were arduous and rather harrowing, but necessary in view of the injuries sustained by aircrew in raids. A few also trained and annotated for rehabilitation duties.

The medical branch, incidentally, gave valuable on-the-spot treatment when a WAAF hostel of Technical training command in London was severely damaged by a flying bomb. There were 70–80 airwomen in the hostel at the time, and several officers were on the fifth floor. None of them were injured, but one woman was discovered with a severed artery. The woman medical officer had already gone straight to her own section, so she could be contacted at once, with the result that the airwoman received immediate first aid, which undoubtedly saved her life. The sick quarters were badly damaged too, but the orderlies were all on duty, with emergency arrangements functioning and ready to deal with casualties.

These were not the only medical trades open to WAAFs. Women were accepted as dispensers, if they held one of the recognized civilian qualifications. At the end of 1944 there were 39 WAAF dispensers. Qualified women were also taken on as masseuses, and 51 of these were serving at the same date. Laboratory assistants, radiographers, chiropodists and operating room assistants were still other specialist medical trades filled by a few WAAFs.

Still in the medical field, the WAAF dental clerk orderlies proved so much better than airmen available that dental officers tried to get 100 per cent replacements. This could not be fully achieved due to the various orders forbidding WAAFs from being posted to a station where there were no other girls, nor to allow one or even two WAAFs to travel around in a mobile surgery. The regulation concerning mobile surgeries was disregarded in some cases, though, notably in No 60 Group, without any world-shattering effects. Many of the orderlies later became dental hygienists and did valuable work. They saved dental officers a lot of time and attracted the clean, careful, intelligent girl.

Safety equipment workers have already been described, their trades including parachute packer, parachute repairer, fabric worker, dinghy packer and repairer. In the end, there were some 2,719 airwomen in these life-saving trades, and as contented a body as any in the WAAF.

Some other trades cannot be fitted into any broad category, but by their very rarity are interesting. Acetylene welders never really got beyond a maximum of eleven girls, all experienced in civilian life. Armourers were always cramped by physical limitation and because no women were permitted to handle lethal weapons. The WAAF armourers hardly ever did any more exciting work than filling ammunition belts.

There was a peak force of 46 shoe repairers. Waitresses, on the other hand, reached the respectable total of 1,000. Although the trade of pigeon keeper was opened to the WAAF, no one was ever mustered into it, unlike the girls in the First World War.

Hairdressers were introduced in 1942. Their work was very good and their salons light and attractive. Bomb plotters and drogue packers were sub-trades introduced into Flying Training Command in 1942. By 1945 the number of officers and airwomen in the Provost branch totalled 49 and 334 respectively.

Five hundred WAAFs were at work at one time as cine-projectionists but in the end most of them found it too monotonous for their temperament. For some reason, too, the number of WAAF photographers never reached great proportions. But as Chapter 9 reveals, the WAAF officers in photographic interpretation did duty that could not have been more vital to victory.

Chapter 8

The Ferry Pilots

L ater in the war, a limited number of WAAFs were accepted for transfer to the Air Transport Auxiliary. This was formed soon after the start of hostilities in 1939. The main purpose of the ATA was to ferry new, repaired or damaged military aircraft between factories, assembly plants and maintenance units and on to active service airfields. Deliveries of aircraft were made to Royal Air Force and Fleet Air Arm, and the aircrew were soon christened 'ferry pilots'.

The first eight women were recruited to this crucial service in January 1940, to be joined by many others, including some seventeen from the WAAF. One of the early ATA women was the legendary aviatrix Amy Johnson, who later lost her life piloting an Oxford twin-engined aircraft, which crashed into the Thames Estuary on 6 January 1941.

During the Battle of Britain and subsequently there developed an increasing need for ferrying new Spitfires and Hurricanes to RAF fighter airfields to replace damaged aircraft and those actually lost. White Waltham became the first HQ of the ATA and the number one ferry pool, but by 1944 the ATA had 22 UK bases, 551 male pilots and 108 female. These were supported by 109 flight engineers of both sexes. And as the Allies eventually advanced across France, Holland and Germany, the peak personnel of ATA reached 3,555, comprising aircrew, ground staff, and RAF and WAAF attached staff. When disbanded in November 1945 the ATA had ferried the astounding number of 309,011 aircraft of all types. A total of 174 highly trained personnel were killed.

Eventually, 166 women served in the ATA, 15 of whom lost their lives. Earlier on, female pilots were only permitted to fly light training aircraft, but this was extended to the twin Battle of Britain fighters – Spitfires and Hurricanes, or 'two matchless fighters' as Douglas Bader called them. Later on too, women ferried Typhoons, twin-engined bombers and even four-engined bombers – the Halifax, Stirling and Lancaster.

It was actually the early months of 1944 before 17 members of the WAAF were transferred for flying training as ATA ferry pilots. And a further six months elapsed until the time when some were assigned to active ferry service. It is difficult to describe the activities and achievements of these 17 WAAF, but they soon acquired a reputation for reliability, sometimes in the face of original male opposition. So the following rather random episodes in their respective air careers represented the exceptional events instead of their daily ferry routine (varied as that certainly was).

Undoubtedly the most remarkable of many emergencies precipitated by the British weather was that of WAAF ferry pilot Betty Keith-Jopp. The Fairey Barracuda had a triple purpose, as torpedo-bomber, dive-bomber and reconnaissance aircraft. Betty was ferrying a Barracuda from Prestwick to Lossiemouth, both in Scotland, when she flew into unexpectedly low clouds. The dim limits of the Firth of Forth became increasingly blurred as the clouds reached ever lower until sky and sea seemed to merge into one and there was not even a hazy horizon.

Betty decided it would be impossibly foolhardy to fly further towards Lossiemouth, so she swung the unwieldy machine round amid the deep grey gloom. She must have been much nearer the water than imagined and she suddenly felt the Barracuda shiver as it struck the Firth.

The torpedo-bomber went down in seconds as Betty began to realize that she might die. Initially, she accepted her likely fate. Two thoughts flashed and pulsed through her brain. This was how Amy Johnson had died in comparable circumstances. Then, the insurance payable on her life would help her mother care for her disabled brother. But then human survival instincts replaced thoughts of mortality. As the Barracuda jarred against the bottom of the Firth, Betty automatically hit the canopy release. A complex series of pressure variations – plus a minor miracle – were at once set in train. As she jettisoned the hood, strong air bubbles precipitated her out of the aircraft and she shot up missile-like to the choppy surface of the Firth of Forth.

She had no life jacket or any other survival tackle, which was perhaps a blessing. The fog clouds blotted out any idea of her location in relation to the shoreline. Also, Betty did not claim to be an exceptional swimmer. The water was icy, but fortuitously she was not wearing heavy clothing or flying boots. She swam around and called for help with as many vocal decibels as her strength allowed. By a second minor miracle, the motor fishing trawler *Provide* was on the Firth and late returning to port, due to earlier engine trouble. Her skipper, David Morris, heard one of her calls and saw a dark form in the water. It was not a seal, as he had imagined. In minutes the *Provide* was alongside Betty and hauling her into the trawler. After a hot drink, they hurried her to Anstruther, where she was stretchered ashore and taken to Crail Fleet Air Arm hospital. Next day, Betty was well enough to get back to her starting point.

Not all ferry pilots were as fortunate as Betty Keith-Jopp. Dora Lang was a WAAF with flying experience before her ferry training. In May 1944, she was piloting a Mosquito. This exciting 400-mph design was made of wood and actually flew Leonard Cheshire the same year in a famous raid on Munich. Tragically, a month or so before this attack, which won Cheshire the Victoria Cross, Dora was ferrying her Mosquito when it crash landed at Lasham airfield, killing the blonde-haired WAAF pilot.

Ferry pilots were vulnerable to mishap from their very first training flights with an instructor. Ruth Russell was airborne with her instructor when they came in to land. He was at the controls as they flew into virtually invisible wires. The trainer aircraft hit the ground soon afterwards. Ruth was hardly hurt but the pilot had a leg badly twisted, which was causing him agony. Eventually an ambulance arrived. Despite this non-reassuring part of Ruth's training, within a year of the accident, she flew solo in her first Spitfire.

After initial pilot training, there followed a score or so of cross-country flights for WAAF ferry pilots to familiarize themselves with some of the conditions anticipated on all ferry flights – and some unexpected ones, too. Frances Rudge took off alone in a Magister when stuttering and spluttering began in the engine at an altitude of a mere 100 feet. The only possible direction for an emergency landing looked to be round to the right, where a hedge marked the limit of this potential landing strip. Frances kept calm, hauled her rudder to the right and managed to land a little short of the hedge. She descended from the Magister to see a group of GIs huddled by the hedge. They had thought she might have come down amongst them!

First postings came after Class I training, when the WAAFs started to ferry trainers and other light aircraft from Tiger Moth to Swordfish. Then, after the next stage, Class II Aircraft flown included the much-sought Spitfire and Hurricane. Yvonne Margaret Eveleigh was one of the best students, so that after the stipulated 50 hours spent with Class I types, she was posted to a Class II course at Thame, where Joyce Fenwick was the only other WAAF on the course. They were taught on the Harvard advanced pilot trainer, a low-slung-wing monoplane with a top speed touching 200 mph.

After Yvonne's first solo, she landed successfully, but then, in a momentary lapse, operated the wrong lever – 'Undercarriage Up' – when she should have chosen 'Flaps Up'. The ground crew had to be summoned to jack up the aircraft to be able to lock the undercarriage for a safe taxi to rest. She received a reprimand for this error, but after subsequent solo Harvard training she was considered fit for a Spitfire. The thrill of this first Spitfire solo remained with her for evermore.

By that winter, Yvonne was ferrying a variety of Class I aircraft and at last came the long-awaited order to collect a Spitfire from North Weald. Waiting at the historic fighter station, Yvonne was asked in the mess why she was there. She still recalled replying, 'I'm collecting a Spit!'

She finally found herself alone in the pilot seat of her Spit and speeding some 400 yards towards take-off. Suddenly the fighter swung off the runway to her right, stopped abruptly in soft mud and tilted nose-first downwards. 'I cursed myself,' she said later, and feared for the worst from officialdom. After a long wait, a control van arrived with an officer aboard. 'Damn bad luck a tyre bursting on take-off like that,' he said. Yvonne was inwardly thrilled that it had not been her fault. The report on the incident read 'Pilot not responsible.' She went on to fly other Spitfires 'without incident'.

At one stage, Sue Alexander and Patricia Provis received a brief posting to Prestwick – that same starting station as Betty Keith-Jopp in her ill-fated Barracuda. During this sojourn in the Scottish winter, Sue travelled to Lossiemouth. She had a date with an elderly Swordfish, Fairey's early stalwart of the Fleet Air Arm. Snow prevented her ferrying the Swordfish from the Lossiemouth runway for a while, but eventually it was cleared to each side of the runway. In the appalling prevailing weather conditions, Sue Alexander was unable to stop the Swordfish aiming straight into one of the snow banks. She acted instantly to switch off engine and petrol, while the Swordfish did a silent and sedate somersault on to its back. Sue was not hurt – simply still earthbound in a loop-the-loop posture. She said later, 'The Swordfish was an old one going to be broken up, but they did not want it broken up on their runway!'

Patricia Provis had Swordfish trouble when she had to accomplish a forced landing near Turnberry airfield. She ended safely at 'what is now I think the ninth hole on Turnberry golf course'.

June Farquhar had a rather different experience at Hawarden when she was marooned there by fog over New Year. This was her moving account of those three days.

'It was a refit station for aircrew who needed to make up a new team for bombers. I landed there in my little Tiger Moth and was adopted by a Wellington crew who had lost their skipper. It was a highly emotional and marvellous time, for one lived for the moment and discounted the lives lost. These wonderful kids made me their skipper for that short duration and we did everything as a team: church on Sunday, parties, the lot. It was desperately sad, they did not last long when back on Ops, but such was life. One had to cope with that and one did.'

Meanwhile, Yvonne Eveleigh was having a busy time at Thame ferry pool. Winter weather still made many trips hazardous. Summarizing one of them, Yvonne had to take a Proctor to Kirkbride. Fog forced her to choose a west-coast route towards the Scottish destination. Yvonne got as far as Barrow before the weather closed in and she had to put down there. Taking off from Barrow next day, Yvonne suffered a potentially dangerous bang, signifying that one of the Proctor's tyres had burst. Eventually, after further delays, she flew on to Kirkbride. Once more the weather forecast for next day was bad, so she decided not to wait for a possible return by air. She caught the night train to London, then another to Aylesbury, and finally got a lift to Thame ferry pool. She had a wash and change of shirt. Then on reporting to operations Yvonne read the chit they handed her. It told her to take an Auster from Aston Down to Kirkbride! She got there after one of her 'bumpiest flights' and then had to take the train south for a second time.

Yvonne then had her first experience of ferrying a Lysander. This Westland-made monoplane was designed for RAF/Army co-operation, but destined to go down into aviation and war history for its poignant part in dropping Allied agents into Europe.

So the role of the ferry pilots went on. The girls always had their precious Ferry Pilots' Notes with them, and in this small blue book they could check on every type of aircraft in use by the RAF and Fleet Air Arm. It must have saved many lives ...

Although small in numbers, the WAAF ferry pilots were proving a crucial constituent of the ATA, which by 1944–1945 had spread explosively as the demands for aircraft grew. The WAAF girls (if that word is permitted) ferried new aircraft from the factories to be fitted out with all the necessities of sophisticated air warfare – radio, armaments, and anything else required for the role of a particular type of plane. Then when the machines were ready, the WAAF flew them to their respective stations. The top ATA pilots might be called on to transport any one of the hundred current designs.

The Hamble ferry pool, between Portsmouth and Southampton, was typical of the many such centres and Yvonne Eveleigh typical of WAAF pilots. So it was not surprising to find her posted to Hamble, where she joined three other WAAF colleagues in a cottage they all shared near the ferry pool. These three were on the nearly all-female staff at Hamble. Yvonne and other WAAF pilots at Hamble had a variety of types to fly: Spitfires, Barracudas, the Firefly Fleet Air Arm fighter, successor to the Fulmar, Mustangs, capable of exceeding 400 mph and thought by many to have been the most effective American fighter of the whole war, and the Hawker Typhoon, another fighter touching the 400-mph maximum mark.

Kathleen Stanley-Smith was at Hamble and once she had to fly an Auster in especially bad weather.

'When I saw an airfield, I landed to find out where I was. I discovered that my airfield was just over the next hill, so I hopped back in my Auster and took off, not bothering to fasten my seat-belt. I had not realized how bumpy it was, and there I was, bouncing around, hitting my head on the roof, unable to take my hands off the stick to do up my seatbelt. I never did that again!'

Meanwhile, Yvonne Eveleigh had a couple of minor shocks when ferrying a Martinet. Shock number one came when she heard a 'horrible crack'. She checked everything she could, but nothing seemed amiss. After that there were no more alarms until she reached her destination airfield of St Eval in Cornwall. Shock number two then hit her. As she began her landing approach, she saw an ambulance and crash tender speeding to the runway. Shaken slightly, Yvonne made a second approach run, but the two emergency vehicles were still there below. She decided to land, which she did quite uneventfully.

It was only then that Yvonne realized why the crash vehicles had been assiduously tracking her. The fabric of the Martinet had, in her words, 'peeled off the underside from the cowling right back to the tail, where it was still firmly attached'. The large strips of canvas must have been flapping wildly behind the plane, and they were probably afraid that it had fouled the rudder or elevator. In point of fact, it had done neither … inspection of the log book revealed that the aircraft had just been repaired after a previous crash and the fabric underneath was new and obviously had not been attached properly.

June Farquhar had a priority order for RAF Benson. The aircraft was the rather unexciting Proctor, but on arrival she found it had been filled with fuel. The control tower then gave June the mysterious message not to switch off the engine and then to vacate her seat to a Royal Air Force pilot, who was accompanied by two unidentifiable girls. Only then did June become aware that these girls were to be flown to France and dropped as Allied agents (so not all such flights were by the legendary Lysander). June found it a 'sobering' experience.

Continuing the catalogue of incidents, Ruth Russell was fully qualified to pilot various types by now, as she was among the first batch of 11 WAAFs for flying training back in February 1944. On one particular job she recalled attempting to land the light Tiger Moth in a high wind and on a high hill. After two tries, on the third she had to accept the help of ground crew to hold the wingtips of the trainer and drag it down the final few feet to earth. Without their weight on the wings, the plane could well have blown away!

Barbara Lankshear, from that same February intake, remembered later the extra-narrow Fleet Air Arm short runways on their airfields. Perhaps the powers that were made these deliberately difficult as a way of preparing pilots for landing on aircraft carriers.

Winifred Stokes and Diana Faunthorpe each took a Swordfish to Northern Ireland, flying over water for the initial time. They were then both approved for Class II training, and after they flew the Harvard in February 1945, notched up their Spitfire solos. These were achieved only three weeks later.

Kathleen Stanley-Smith also recalled her maiden Spitfire solo. She took off easily, but not before she had had to wait for the fighter's Rolls-Royce Merlin engine to cool down after another pilot's flight on a hot day. This delay had a delayed effect on Kathleen's nerves. The result was that she suddenly felt unable to land. On each approach she got down to within yards of the runway and then opened up and flew a further circuit before her next attempt. Eventually the flight captain took control of the situation and got her to land securely no fewer than three more times.

After this course, WAAF pilots were promoted to First Officers. Annette Mahon, in contrast to Kathleen, found more trouble taking off than landing. As an example of the versatility demanded of all ferry pilots at this more advanced stage, Ruth Russell chalked up a remarkable further 14 diverse types to be flown often at minimum notice. By the beginning of May 1945 and hearing the end of the war in Europe, Ruth was ferrying from Sherburn-in-Elmet. She flew Spitfires, Barracudas, Spitfire Mk IX, Reliant, Martinet, Hellcat, Hurricanes Mk II and IV, Mustangs and Firefly. Then she had to prove herself familiar with the Wildcat (American fighter for aircraft-carriers), Seafire (Fleet Air Arm's version of the Spitfire), Corsair (first US fighter to fly faster than 400 mph in level flight) and the Sea Otter (not quite so fast).

VE-Day, 8 May 1945, seemed to arrive quite suddenly. It was time for the WAAFs to celebrate. Although they might not have been flying for very long, most of them had served in the WAAF for the majority of the war. Yvonne happened to be on short leave at the time of the German surrender. She went up to London where she met WAAF friends and gathered outside Buckingham Palace. Unable to find anywhere to sleep that night, Yvonne tried the Overseas League, where she was a member. The night porter let her sleep on a couch there, and even awoke her with a cup of tea.

The war went on against Japan, but the Air Transport Auxiliary was bound to be in less demand. Yet meanwhile, the ferry pilots were still kept busy on such jobs as picking up Spitfires and other fighters for breaking up or other disposal. One such Spitfire bore 14 crosses representing the number of enemy aircraft destroyed. The Women's Pool at Hamble was soon to be closed, though not before a celebratory party. WAAFs wanting to stay in the service as long as possible were posted elsewhere, and Yvonne went to Whitchurch, Bristol, with Veronica Volkers.

Aimee de Neve was sent to the Ratcliffe ferry pool. The airfield there belonged to Sir Lindsey Everard, and before the war was a flying club. Ratcliffe had a number of highly experienced pilots, both male and female. June Farquhar was one of a dozen pilots billeted at Ratcliffe Hall with Sir Lindsey and Lady Everard. While there they actually met Mr Churchill several times at dinner, as well as the legendary aviation pioneer Frederick Handley Page. His name is forever associated with the Halifax and Hampden bombers.

Perhaps the single most significant incident conveying the work and dangers of ferry pilots occurred to Kathleen Stanley-Smith just before final victory. She was also flying from Ratcliffe, when it became her turn to fly the so-called taxi Fairchild.

'I took off with three passengers for a factory airfield just east of Birmingham. I delivered them and took off again so as to meet them at their destination. At approximately 300 feet the engine failed. Our training when that happened on take-off was to land straight ahead . . . but straight ahead there was nothing but the rooftops of Birmingham. I did a 180-degree turn back to the airfield. The engine kicked in for a few moments, which helped, then quit for good. I missed the hangar roof by inches, and then did a heavy landing on the grass, breaking the undercarriage and tipping on my nose. Firm ground never felt so good, and I still have the tip of that prop!'

Kathleen married an American and became Mrs Hirsch. Most of the WAAF ferry pilots left the ATA that autumn. A final air display at White Waltham was flown in aid of dependants of the many ATA pilots killed. And by the end of November all the ATA ferry pools were closed. While serving in ATA, Frances Rudge and Joyce also married, Frances's husband nearly being killed in an air crash. Yvonne Eveleigh and Rosemary Bonnet both lost pilot husbands earlier in the war, before they joined ATA. Apart from Dora Lang there were no other fatalities among WAAF ferry pilots. This was remarkable testimony to the WAAFs themselves and their instructors. Ferry pilots flew aircraft that were unarmed, often without radio and vulnerable to enemy attack. The ATA as a whole lost over 100 pilots.

Chapter 9

The V-Weapons

This is the amazing story of the battle against the V-weapons, told by Constance Babington Smith, a WAAF flight officer working with Photographic Intelligence. Much has already been said and written about the Vergeltung weapons both from the German and from the Allied viewpoints. It ranges all the way from the preliminary propaganda about Wunderwaffen, and from certain equally exaggerated post-war clams for the Allied countermeasures to official histories and authoritative first-hand accounts. There is much, however, that has never been published. Almost every account of the V-weapon battle of wits alludes to the major part played by photographic intelligence in analyzing and assessing the threat, but the full extent of its role and the great variety of ways in which it helped have hitherto been kept secret.

Photographic intelligence was, I need hardly say, only one of many complementary sources of information. The agents who risked their lives in Germany and the occupied countries, the interrogators who questioned the prisoners of war, the men and women who combed through trade magazines and monitored German broadcasts, the technical experts who examined V-weapon fragments: these were only a few of the vast incongruous team that supplied the raw material of the investigation. Finally, at the top, there were the intelligence experts who weighed all the varied evidence and upon whose judgement depended what action was likely to be taken.

'The story that I have to tell is not the story of how photographic intelligence solved the V-weapon mystery single handed, without missing a single clue; it is, rather, a strangely paradoxical story of conspicuous successes and conspicuous failures. At certain stages it brought to the overall intelligence picture a rapid accuracy and precision, and also a wideness of vision that simply could not have existed otherwise; while at others, all the skill and perseverance of both pilots and interpreters were completely fruitless.

'On 15 May 1942, Flight Lieutenant DW Steventon flew in his Spitfire high above the western shores of the Baltic, on the way to cover Swinemünde after photographing Kiel. Far below and ahead lay the island of Usedom, with its long belt of woodland facing the Baltic, and separated from the mainland by the River Peene. He happened to notice that there was an airfield at the northern tip of the island, with quite a lot of new developments nearby, and he switched on his camera for a short run.

'At Medmenham, the Second Phase interpreters puzzled over some strange, massive ring-like things in the woods near the airfield, and they worked out the pinpoint and noted down "heavy constructional work", and then turned their attention to destroyers off Swinemünde. The sortie then went on to the Third Phase section as usual, for interpretation on different specialized subjects. I remember flipping through the stack of photographs and deciding the scale was too small to make it worthwhile looking at the aircraft. Then something unusual caught my eye, and I stopped to take a good look at some extraordinary circular embankments. I glanced quickly at the plot to see where it was, and noticed the name Peenemünde. Then I looked at the prints again. "No," I thought to myself, "those don't belong to me. I wonder what on earth they are. Somebody must know all about them, I suppose." And I then dismissed the whole thing from my mind. But when the sortie finished its rounds, no one had staked a claim for the mysterious "rings" at Peenemünde, and the cardboard boxes full of photographs were set in place on a shelf in the print library, for future reference when required. There the matter rested, as far as Medmenham was concerned, for the next seven months.

'Meantime, as we now know, General Dornberger and Wernher von Braun were working day and night at their rockets, and the first fully successful launching of an A-4 rocket – later known as the V2 – took place at the experimental station in the woods on 3 October 1942, while in December an early version of the flying boat, the V1, was launched from below a large aircraft over Peenemünde.

'In that same December reports of "secret weapon trials" in this area began reaching London and began to cause concern. The fact that the Germans were developing long-range weapons was already known to British intelligence, for a communication known as the "Oslo Report", giving advance information on plans for new weapons, including rockets, had reached London via Oslo as early as the autumn of 1939. But like those first photographs of Peenemünde that Steventon took by chance in 1942, the "Oslo Report" had been filed away for future reference when required.

'By the beginning of 1943 there was a large and thriving section of Army interpreters at Medmenham, which ministered to the needs of the War Office in matters of photographic intelligence. In February, Major Norman Falcon, the officer in charge of this section, was warned by the War Office that the enemy was planning to operate "some form of long-range projectors, capable of firing on this country from the French coast". If this were really true, it meant a weapon of a new order. So photographic evidence relating to it might well be something very unusual. Peenemünde! What about that "heavy constructional work" that had meant nothing to anyone the year before? Soon a further briefing came from the War Office, where it had been calculated that a rocket capable of reaching London from the French coast would have to be launched from a sharply inclined projector about 100 yards long.

'Falcon's interpreters, with several new covers of Peenemünde to work on, prepared a detailed statement. They reported a huge elliptical embankment and three circular earth banks "not unlike empty reservoirs". These were facts that could not be denied, but they did not in the least tally with the hypothesis of a projector 100 yards long. Nothing seemed to tally with anything.

'Such was the embryonic stage of British intelligence on "secret weapons" when, early in April 1943, the evidence was presented to the Chiefs of Staff. But it was convincing enough to bring about the appointment of an investigator-in-chief, Mr Duncan Sandys, then Joint Parliamentary Secretary to the Minister of Supply. The Chiefs of Staff, and the Prime Minister himself, were taking the "secret weapon" threat seriously enough to be determined to find out just how serious it was.

'Repercussions of Mr Sandys's appointment were felt immediately. The Air Ministry at once instructed Group Captain Peter Stewart (then Station Commander at Medmenham) to institute a secret weapon investigation on the highest priority. Wing Commander Hamshaw Thomas, who by this time was directing all Third Phase work, was put in charge, while an interpreter named Flight Lieutenant Andre Kenny and three others were assigned to search for clues of experimental work and production, especially at Peenemünde. At the same time Norman Falcon and two of his Arm interpreters were to concentrate on the military side of the investigation, which meant primarily watching potential launching areas on the French coast. Meanwhile, a special flying programme was laid on – shared by Benson and the Americans at Mount Farm – to ensure that every square mile of the French coastal area from Cherbourg to the Belgian frontier had been photographed since the beginning of the year.

'So the photographic search for secret weapons began in earnest in April 1943. No one really quite knew what they were looking for, although the Air Ministry did suggest that the interpreters should be on the lookout for three things: a long-range gun, a remotely controlled rockets aircraft and "some sort of tube located in a disused mine out of which a rocket could be squirted".

'On 29 April, Andre Kenny set off for the Ministry of Supply to report what had so far been found at Peenemünde. With Mr Sandys were his scientific advisers, two of whom had recently spent a whole day at Medmenham. Kenny spread out plans of the whole area so that Mr Sandys could see the lie of the land and showed him that all the main installations were at the northern end of the island of Usedom. He drew attention to the rig power station at Kolpin, near the village of Peenemünde, with power lines radiating throughout the experimental station, and he explained the likely functions of the huge new workshops among the trees. There must obviously be plans for large-scale production of some kind. Then he pointed out the airfield further north, with its neat row of hangars, and beyond it some reclamation work indicating that the landing area was going to be extended. Then all eyes returned to the focal point of interest, the monumental "earthworks" in the woods, and Kenny produced enlargements and more plans. He explained how he had come to the conclusion that the structures within some of the earthworks might well be test stands for launching missiles.

'This was the first time that Mr Sandys had come into touch with a photographic interpreter, and he was much surprised and impressed by the amount of detailed information the photographs could yield. Before the meeting broke up he was firmly convinced that the whole Peenemünde site was an experimental station and that its circular and elliptical earthworks were probably for testing rockets.

'On 9 May 1943, Mr Sandys visited Medmenham, where he first talked with the Army interpreters and with Kenny in the Industrial Section. Then he came on to the Aircraft Section, as at this stage he was concerning himself with the search for a "remotely controlled pilotless aircraft" as well as with rockets proper. He questioned me as to whether I had seen any aircraft at Peenemünde that I could not identify, but at this point there was nothing helpful I could say. None of the existing covers was sharp enough or of large enough scale to give the sort of information that was needed. However, from then on I knew that the airfield had to be carefully watched.

'Four times in June Peenemünde was photographed. The first cover, taken on 2 June, was a good clear one, and Kenny could report quite a lot of new detail, including a "thick vertical column about 40 feet high" on a fan-shaped stretch of open foreshore. And then on 23 June Flight Sergeant EPH Peel came back with photographs that were exceptionally good. Flying in his Mosquito high over the experimental station he had been completely unaware how much was going on down below in the brilliant June sunshine, but back at Medmenham there was plenty for Hamshaw Thomas and Kenny to feast their eyes on. Two rockets – actual rockets – had been photographed, lying horizontally, on road vehicles within the confines of the elliptical earthwork, and even today, that superbly clear photograph makes it easy to imagine the stab of elation Kenny must have felt when he saw them.

'The setting was clear in every detail too. Above the rockets towered a structure resembling a massive observation tower, and the steep encircling slope of the earthwork might have been some sinister Germanic stadium. Beyond the great oval were the woods and seawards, at the end of an approach road, there was the fan-shaped stretch of foreshore.

'Kenny's cautiously worded report described "torpedo-like objects thirty-eight feet long", but by the time the news had been rushed to the Prime Minister they had been definitely labelled as rockets. And within the next few days Mr Churchill directed that photographic intelligence should be enabled by every possible means to make a maximum contribution to the secret weapon investigation.

'It was at this point, in June 1943, that I myself was first able to say something positive about the experimental work at Peenemünde, for on the same sortie that showed those first rockets there were several runs over the airfield. My brief was to watch for "anything queer", and the four little tailless aeroplanes that I found taking the air on 23 June looked queer enough to satisfy anybody. This was the first time I was able to analyze and measure the Messerschmitt liquid-rocket fighter, the Me 163 (which we provisionally named 'Peenemünde 30'), but it was not the first time it had been photographed at Peenemünde, as I found out within a few hours by turning up all the previous covers.

'The process of going back over earlier photographs was something that was happening the entire time in the V-weapon investigation. For the sequence of photographic flights and of interpretation finds did not run smoothly parallel to the sequence of what was actually happening on the German ground. That is not the way that photographic intelligence works. Each new find was likely to throw more light on earlier photographs, which had meant nothing when they were first examined. So quite apart from the normal time lag between the date of actual photography and the date of the interpreter's report, "first photographed" and "first seen" often did not refer to the same cover at all.

'So it was in the case of my tailless aircraft. Peenemünde airfield had been photographed eleven times before 23 June, but almost all the covers were of small scale and poor quality and I had tried in vain to find anything useful to say about those woolly looking photographs. It had been peering through an overlay of tracing paper – you could see blurred shapes but you couldn't possibly even hint what they were. But now that I had actually seen the tailless aircraft, and knew which buildings they frequented, I could go back to those earlier "bits of dotting paper" and pick out pale blurred little shapes, which almost certainly represented the strange flying machines. The photographs taken on 23 June also showed the first "jet marks" I had ever recognized – single, dark, fan-shaped marks, from which dark streaks led out across the airfield – and in this case also I was able to go back and identify earlier streaks.

'Duncan Sandys had already reported to the War Cabinet that the development of jet-propelled aircraft was probably proceeding side by side with the work on rockets and "airborne rocket torpedoes". The photographs of the "Peenemünde 30" definitely confirmed this although we now know, of course, that it did not have any direct bearing on the secrets of the V1 and the V2.

'Meanwhile the photographs of northern France were providing ominous evidence. Early in July a ground report had reached London linking secret weapon activity with a village name Watten near Calais. Two months earlier the Army interpreters had reported on a clearing in the woods near Watten, but the spot had not been photographed since. This was quickly remedied, and the new cover showed that a great deal had happened in the interval. Work was well ahead on what was clearly going to be some gigantic concrete structure. Suspicious looking preliminaries were also going ahead at two other places in the rocket range area, and all three sites were rail-served from main lines – a fact to which many of the British rocket experts attached great importance. For by this time they were talking of 40-ton or 45-ton rockets, and missiles of this weight would have to be brought to their launching sites by rail. These theories, however, were by no means universally accepted. Lord Cherwell, in particular, could not bring himself to believe that a 40-ton rocket was a feasible proposition. He felt that a pilotless aircraft described in one of the ground reports as "an air mine with wings" was much more likely to be an immediate danger.

'Both in London and at Medmenham it was a time of frustrating confusion in the secret weapon investigation, which by now had been given the codename Bodyline – a time of groping in the dark, of trying to lay foundations in a swamp. It was as though the parts of two or three jigsaw puzzles had been jumbled together, and it was surely tempting to try to find only one answer, only one weapon. It seemed a triumph when two or three bits of puzzle fitted together and could be identified as "Rocket", as it was all too easy to ignore the bits that did not fit in with these.

'In spite of the conflicting views about rockets, however, Duncan Sandys was convinced that the secret weapon threat was a grave one. Soon after, the decision was made to attack Peenemünde. On the night of 17 August 1943, when Bomber Command made their famous raid, forty aircraft were lost, but considerable destruction was caused. We know now that it seriously delayed the whole V2 programme, though estimates of just how long a delay it caused vary from four weeks to six months.

'Then ten days later, on 27 August, the US Eighth Air Force attacked Watten. The attack on the "launching shelter" for V2s, as General Dornberger called it, could not possibly have been better timed, for a huge mass of concrete was in the process of hardening when the bombs came down, and within a day or two a chaotic jumble of steel props, and planking was utterly rigid and immovable. Sir Malcolm McAlpine, the eminent engineer, who was asked to comment on the damage assessment photographs, said, "It would be easier to start over again." According to General Dornberger, the German engineer in charge shared his view.

'During the spring and summer of 1943 there had been two main currents of V-weapon interpretation at Medmenham: the work of Kenny and his helpers, concerned chiefly with Peenemünde itself; and that of the Army interpreters under Norman Falcon and his second-in-command Captain Neil Simon, who struggled to make sense out of the early developments at Watten and the other "heavy sites" in France. In September there was a readjustment of responsibility. Douglas Kendall was given direction of the whole investigation by Hamshaw Thomas, and Norman Falcon agreed that the Army interpreters involved should expand the scope of their work to include all types of possible V-weapon activity.

Kendall was by this tine a Wing Commander and in charge of Second Phase, the model making section, the topographical reporting and much else: in the daytime he never had a moment for interpretation, but when evening came he always gravitated towards the Army Section, eager to see any new Bodyline finds, any new "unidentified activity", any trees being felled in the woods of the Pas-de-Calais, any dumps of building materials in the little valleys of the Cherbourg Peninsula, and especially any signs of new railway spurs.

'Almost every day there were sinister new activities to be examined. Near Mimoyecques, not far from Cap Gris Nez, a new railway spur was being tunnelled right through a hill, and was surrounded by three phoney "haystacks", which might very well hide nearly vertical shafts. This might tie in with those peculiar rumours of rockets that were going to be squirted up from underground, but what more could one say? At Sottevast and Martinvast, near Cherbourg, there were burrowings and scrapings and new railway spurs; and at Siracourt, Lottinghem, and Wigernes, between Calais and the Somme, the same sort of goings on, but all at such an early stage that they might develop into almost anything.

'In retrospect it is not surprising that the heavy sites were so hard to understand, for they were not, in fact, a related system of launching sites for a single type of weapon. Four of them were intended as "launching shelters" for V2s; two as mammoth launching sites for V1s; and Mimoyecques was to have housed a multi-barrelled long-range gun, which never materialized at all.

'At the Ministry of Supply, on 21 October, Duncan Sandys decided the rocket danger was so grave that the whole suspect area must be rephotographed. For the third time a flying programme involving about 100 separate sorties was laid on: 100 separate sorties each consisting of hundreds of photographs, every one of which had to be scanned with care. During the first week of November the full effects of this hit Medmenham. Each day the box files stacked up in towering mountains around the Army interpreter whose job it was to watch France: Captain Robert Rowell. Doggedly he ploughed through the piles of prints, searching for railways spurs and for scratchings and burrowings that had not been there before. It was not yet a hunt for actual rockets, of course, but it was very definitely a hunt for rocket launching sites –rail-served rocket launching sites.

'Into this rocket-conscious atmosphere there came suddenly, on 4 November 1943, a major new discovery, which at first did not seem to fit in anywhere. On the contrary, it merely seemed to add a new complication. A few days earlier a report had reached London from an agent in France, telling that the construction firm he worked for was engaged on building eight "sites" in the Pas-de-Calais, not far from Abbeville. He could not understand what they were for, though he strongly suspected they had to do with secret weapons, but he could describe exactly what they were. On 3 November the eight places in question were photographed.

'When the specially flown sorties arrived at Medmenham Neil Simon offered to lend a hand, as Rowell was already swamped with work. Later they puzzled together over what they had found – in some disappointment. There was something "starting" all right at each of the eight pinpoints, and it was evidently the same "something" in each case. But there was no railway anywhere near, let alone new rail spurs leading to the sites.

'Late that evening, when Douglas Kendall got back from a day's meetings in London, he made straight for the Army Section. With Simon and Rowell he looked quickly at each of the eight sites, each one partly in a wood, and each apparently to have a set of nine standard buildings, some of them strangely shaped. Then he settled down to gaze at the site, which was furthest advanced, near Yvranch, in a wood called Bois Carré. Three of the buildings were unlike anything he had even seen in his life. Except – yes – they *were* like something. They took his mind back to winter sports before the war, for they reminded him of skis. "Skis," he thought aloud. "That's what they look like – skis." Two of them seemed to be identical, and the third was shorter; and each, in plain view, had one gently curving end. They were like a giant's skis laid down on their sides.

'Through the early hours of the morning the Bodyline interpreters measured and checked, compared and discussed. Each clearing and each pit, each dump of building materials, each semi-complete building, each road and path was analyzed from the viewpoint of the overriding question of the day: "What is the connection with rockets?" At the end of it all, the answer was inconclusive. These new sites might be for launching projectiles of some sort, but they bore no relation to anything else that had been found so far.

'When the report on these eight curious sites reached its recipients in London, it added no fuel to the flames of controversy that were raging more fiercely than ever in Bodyline circles. These new sites, whatever they might be intended for, were apparently not for rockets. The two schools of thought about secret weapons that had grown up during the past six months were by now coming into conflict. Duncan Sandys himself led the group, which believed that the long-range rocket was the only weapon that really mattered; while the others, including Lord Cherwell, stuck to their guns in differing from him. There were one or two scientists in this group who even maintained that Peenemünde was a gigantic hoax and that the rockets photographed there were dummies. Things reached such an impasse that the Prime Minister himself intervened. He appointed Sir Stafford Cripps, then Minister of Aircraft Production, to examine the facts and decide whether the German secret weapons really existed at all, and if so what was the nature and extent of the threat. A meeting was called for the morning of 8 November 1943 at which the primary evidence was to be examined.

'In the conference room at the Cabinet Offices Sir Stafford Cripps sat at the head of the great U-shaped table, and on either side of him was a splendid array of Generals and Admirals and Air Marshals, as well as Duncan Sandys representing the Prime Minister and a train of distinguished scientific advisers. At one side of the table, in the bottom three places, were Douglas Kendall, Neil Simon and Andre Kenny.

'The first evidence to be presented consisted of reports from agents and other secret sources. It was, on the whole, vague and lacking detail. Some of it referred to rockets, but there were also allusions to pilotless aircraft. Then came an analysis of German propaganda, which tended to confirm the existence of German secret weapons, but only in an indirect manner.

'It is a startling thought that those first witnesses gave the sum total of primary evidence from sources other than aerial photographs. If no such thing as photographic reconnaissance had existed, and if the interpreters had not been waiting at the bottom of the table, those vague ground reports and the analysis of propaganda would have been the only basis for Sir Stafford Cripps's judgement. The opening stages of the meeting can, indeed, be compared to the opening stages of the meeting that once took place in ancient Babylon, in the days of Belshazzar the king. There, all the king's wise men could not read the writing or make known to the king the interpretation thereof.

'As it was, however, the better part of the meeting at the Cabinet Office was given over to discussing the photographic evidence. First of all Kenny spoke about Peenemünde, the rockets that had been seen there and the effects of the RAF attack. Then the questioning switched to Watten and the other heavy sites in France. Kendall described what had been found at each. At last there was a pause, but Sir Stafford had one more question.

'"Apart from the heavy sites, have you any other information to suggest secret weapon activity in northern France?"

'"Yes," replied Kendall, "we have."

'The attention of the meeting, which had been wilting somewhat as one heavy site after another was discussed, was suddenly electrified. There was breathless silence as Sir Stafford asked, "What have you found?"

'"A new sort of installation, almost certainly a launching site of some kind. A whole system of them is being built in the Pas-de-Calais."

"'How many are there?'"

"'Up to midnight last night we'd found nineteen.'"

"'Nineteen!' echoed round the table.

"'Probably more have been found by now," went on Kendall. "We've only had time to search part of the Bodyline area."

"'Why do you think they have anything to do with secret weapons?' asked Sir Stafford.

"'They are not like any known military installation," explained Kendall, "and they all started at once. And each of them is apparently going to have a firing-point aimed at London."

'Sir Stafford immediately decided to adjourn the meeting for two days, so as to give the interpreters a day and two nights to complete their search for the new sites, and to prepare a detailed analysis. By the time the meeting reassembled on 10 November a total of twenty-six "ski sites" had been found. But no clues had yet been discovered to show what sort of missile they were meant for. In the report, which Sir Stafford Cripps submitted to the War Cabinet a few days later, however, he judged that pilotless aircraft were a more immediate danger than long-range rockets. He also advised that photographic cover of Peenemünde and of the danger area in France should be kept up.

'The "Stafford Cripps meeting" helped to cause a general shake-up in Bodyline. Duncan Sandys's special investigation came to an end, though he continued to advise on rockets, and on 18 November the responsibility both for intelligence and for planning countermeasures passed to the Air Staff.

'A fortnight after the meeting no fewer than ninety-five ski sites had been identified. The vast majority were in the Pas-de-Calais, with their firing points on the "London line", but there were also groups in the Cherbourg peninsula aiming at Plymouth and Bristol.

"'We've got to find out what they're for and how they work," said Kendall to Falcon one evening as they returned to the Army Section after dinner in the Mess. "I don't feel we've really proved yet that they're not for rockets." They were joined by Robert Rowell and Neil Simon, and four of them, surrounded by a sea of photographs, plunged once more into argument and counterargument.

"'If the 'sky buildings' really are for storage, which seems the most likely thing," began Falcon, "the shape and size of the things to be stored in them is fairly limited."

'Kendall put the latest cover of the Bois Carré site under a stereoscope, and gazed yet again at the absurdly long flat-roofed windowless buildings. They were nearly 260 feet long, but their width was only just 10 feet.

"'What we've got to check," he said, "is the radius of curvature at the entrance, so as to make sure whether a rocket could be moved in and out."

"'I've calculated that a 38-foot rocket, like the ones at Peenemünde, could just be manoeuvred into a ski building," said Simon, "at least without its fins on."

'Perhaps that was why the third ski building was always shorter than the other two, thought Kendall. It might be for the smaller components of the rocket.

"'So there are no grounds for ruling out rockets as far as the actual ski buildings are concerned," he said. "But I think the firing points are a different story."

'He set in position a different air of photographs, which showed the furthest advanced of the oblong platforms, and his eyes fastened on the platform's narrow extension on which was a row of two-foot upright concrete studs – six pairs of them, twenty feet apart, like a set of buttons down the front of a double-breasted coat.

"'Yes," agreed Falcon, "I think so too. Because if you were going to put up an apparatus for launching rockets at a steep angle, you wouldn't start by making a platform with a long row of concrete studs."

"'Those studs are just the sort of foundations you'd need", put in Rowell, "if you were going to set up steel posts to support something like a bridge."

"'A bridge," repeated Kendall. "Perhaps something like an inclined bridge."

"'In other words, a ramp," remarked Falcon, "and that wouldn't be any use at all for launching rockets, because if you launched a rocket at such a low angle it would fall to the ground almost at once."

"'But if the thing had wings to give it a lift," argued Kendall, "then you would want to launch it from a ramp and not vertically."

'"You couldn't get a missile with wings round the corners of the ski building," Simon pointed out.

'There was silence for about a minute.

'"What about the very small concrete building at the other end of the platform from the studs?" Rowell asked Kendall. "Have you any ideas about that?"

'Kendall laughed. "Don't you think that's for the gentleman who presses the button?" he said. "An interesting job, no doubt, but judging by the strength and the shape of the building, I should think it might be a bit uncomfortable at times."

'They went on to discuss a square building, which in every case was placed exactly in line with the firing-point. Kendall turned up some low obliques of the Bois Carré site, which showed the square building very clearly, with its wide entrance facing towards London.

'"What was the width of the door?" he asked Simon.

'"Twenty-two feet across."

'"Twenty-two. Hmm. So just supposing the missile had its wings put on to it in this building, its wingspan would have to be less than twenty-two feet. Right?"

'"And if the wings weren't put on till the last minute," added Falcon, "the components could be stored in the ski buildings."

'"But why should the square building be so carefully oriented to London?" said Kendall. "It must be something to do with setting directional control. The missile could have a dramatically directed automatic pilot I suppose."

'Before the end of November Kendall had issued a report suggesting that the missile to be fired from the ski sites was a flying bomb. He also described in detail the likely firing procedure. But his seemingly overconfident interpretation was not immediately accepted by some who were still thinking in terms of rockets. On 1 December Douglas Kendall, accompanied once more by Neil Simon, was summoned to an intelligence meeting at the Cabinet Offices, to try to justify his theories and claims.

'I must now go back a little, to describe the stage my own work was reaching on the sidelines of the secret weapon investigation.

First I would emphasize that until November 1943 my contact with Bodyline consisted of two things only: my brief to watch Peenemünde airfield for "anything queer", and my discovery and analysis of the "Peenemünde 30" and the marks it left on the ground. I had no idea that Kenny had found rockets, I knew nothing of the "Stafford Cripps meeting" and the name "ski site" would have had no meaning for me – if I had ever heard it.

'On 13 November, however, Kendall came and asked me to search afresh at Peenemünde for an aircraft, which might be pilotless. My interest in the secret weapon hunt had been flagging a bit, but Kendall's enthusiasm revived it, especially as he gave me something specific to look for: a very small aircraft, smaller than a fighter. This was the first time I had been briefed in these terms. Something smaller than a fighter would only show up on good photographs, so I went to the print library and fetched the famous set of photographs on which I had earlier found the "Peenemünde 30s". It was by far the best of the early covers, and, sure enough, I did find a midget aircraft on those splendid photographs. The absurd little object was not on the airfield, but sitting in a corner of a small enclosure some way behind the hangars, immediately adjoining a building, which I suspected, from its design, was used for testing jet engines. Similar buildings had recently been put up at several of the German aero-engine factories. I named it "Peenemünde 20", as its span was about 20 feet, but there was precious little I could say about it. The midget aircraft had the aggravating cotton wool look that all light-coloured or shiny objects acquire on aerial photographs, owing to the "light spread" that blots out shadow and prevents detailed interpretation, and also makes things look deceptively larger than they are. But Kendall, and also Golovine at the Air Ministry, seemed certain that the "Peenemünde 20" was very important, and they urged me to continue my search. So during the next two weeks I got out more back covers, intent on probing into all the most unlikely corners.

'It so happened that while this search was in progress, on the morning of 28 November 1943, a Mosquito was on its way across the North Sea from Scotland to try for "DA" cover of Berlin. It was a time of steady bad weather over central Europe, and a whole series of attempts to photograph Berlin had failed. The pilot was Squadron Leader John Merifield, who since Alistair Taylor went missing was quietly emerging as the steadiest and most talented of the Mosquito pilots at Leuchars. It was Merifield (when war broke out he was a nineteen-year-old undergraduate at Oxford) who in March 1942 had flown the first cover of Königsberg – a landmark of great significance, as for the first time the whole of northern Germany was within range.

'Merifield and his navigator, Flying Officer Whalley, approached the Berlin area from the north, but when they reached the city they realized that they would not be able to take any photographs there. The cloud was solid below them. Merifield knew, however, that it was much clearer on the Baltic coast, as they had come in that way. So he turned northwards and set course for the alternative targets that had been picked for him at briefing. There were some shipping targets at Stettin and Swinemünde, a flock of airfields, a suspected radar installation at Zinnowitz on the island of Usedom, and various other odd jobs. One after another Merifield photographed them. After Zinnowitz there was still some film left, and Merifield always made a point of using up every scrap. What targets were left? The airfield at Peenemünde. That would just about do it. Flying westwards Merifield switched on his cameras as he reached the northern tip of Usedom, and they clicked away as he crossed the airfield. Then home!

'Three days later, on 1 December, while Kendall was arguing his case at the meeting in London, explaining step by step why he believed so strongly that the ski sites were for launching flying bombs, I was still combing Peenemünde for midgets. There was by this time a big accumulation of back covers, and re-examining them was an undertaking of some magnitude.

'The fact that I had found the "Peenemünde 20" near a building I thought was an engine test-house led me to cast my eyes further afield than usual, towards the no-man's-land which lay between the area I was officially watching and the woods that marked the edge of the main experimental station – the domain of the Industry and Army Sections. There were four rather fancy modern buildings set by themselves in the open here, which I saw sure housed some sort of dynamometer test beds. I had made a close study of test beds, because Walt Rostow and the American target experts had wanted to know the numbers at each German factory as evidence of potential output. I had consulted with authorities on the subject at Farnborough and the Ministry of Aircraft Production as well as at one of the Rolls-Royce factories, and I did not think anyone at Medmenham would contest my right to appropriate these buildings at Peenemünde. I checked the activity near them from cover to cover, and surprisingly, I thought, I did find one crumb of evidence to link then with the "Peenemünde 20". On several dates there was an object resembling a midget airframe outside one of them.

'This first excursion beyond the official bounds of the airfield encouraged me to try my luck in other directions, and I decided to follow the dead straight road, which led northwards along the eastern boundary of the airfield towards the Baltic shore. I passed the limits of the airfield and went on towards the extreme edge of the island. To the right lay an untouched stretch of marshy foreland, but on the left there was a great deal going on – the long-term project of land reclamation for extending the airfield. I could see the plumes of smoke from the bucket-ladder dredgers chugging away offshore, and there were several suction dredgers with their long spidery pipes straggling over the huge semicircle of land which showed up with the hard black and white of constructional work against the settled greys of the airfield and its surroundings.

'I was not in the least interested in the dredging or the land reclamation, which anyway did not "belong" to me. There was a separate section at Medmenham whose sole job was to watch and report on developments at airfields. So I ignored the portentous reclamation scheme, and pursued the straight road leading to the water's edge. Right at the end of the road was something I did not understand, unlike anything I had ever seen before.

'Charles Sims was working at the other side of the room, and I said to him, "Do come and have a look at something here." Sims came over and looked, but like me he was completely nonplussed by the unusual structure I had stumbled upon. I bent down again over the photographs.

'"Surely," I said to Sims, "this is the sort of thing you would put up if you wanted to launch something out to sea, isn't it?" Rumours of "launching rails" for secret weapons had reached me earlier, and ever since I had been briefed about pilotless aircraft. I had been on the lookout for a catapult of some kind.

'I pondered over the photographs and reviewed what I had found. There were four of these strange structures. Three of them looked very much like the sort of cranes that have a box for the operator and a long movable arm. But the fourth seemed different, and it was the one that drew my attention most. It was evidently a sort of ramp banked up with earth – you could tell that from the shadow supporting rails that inclined upwards towards the water's edge. "I'd better check with the Industry interpreters," was my first thought. "They probably know all about these things already." So I took the prints along to the Industry Section, and was told that these "things" had been looked at long ago, and interpreted as something to do with the dredging equipment.

'Back at my desk I gazed at the photographs again. "I don't believe it," I thought. "I must show them to Kendall." So I phoned his office. Kendall was in London, I was told, and might not be back till fairly late. I asked that the moment he arrived he should be told I would like to see him.

'I knew there was a new cover of Peenemünde, flown on 28 November, but I had no right to claim the photographs before the various section with higher priorities, late in the afternoon. However, I said to Ursula Kay, "Do try and get that new cover of Peenemünde," and off she went to track it down.

'Then the door opened. I looked up expecting to see Ursula, but it was Douglas Kendall, still with his coat on, and carrying his briefcase. He looked a bit white and tired, I thought.

'"I hear you want to see me, Babs," he said.

'"Yes, I do. I want you to look at something I've found at Peenemünde. Don't you think it might be a catapult for pilotless aircraft?"

'I showed him one of the single prints, and he was so silent for a minute that I thought he must share the views of the Industry Section.

'Then he said; "That's it! Let's see the pair," and he quickly set my stereoscope over the two photographs. I couldn't understand why he was immediately so certain.

'"You think it is for launching pilotless aircraft then?" I asked.

'"I know it is." He took up the photographs. "I'll just take these along to the Army section. You can have them back soon."

'He was gone before Ursula returned, proudly carrying a box file. Together she and I looked at the plot, and my chief anxiety was as to whether the run over Peenemünde airfield started in time to include the launching place. Fortunately it did – just. Only the first print of the run showed it, and there was no stereo pair. The quality of the photograph was poor, but even with the naked eye I could see that on the ramp was something that had not been there before: a tiny cruciform shape, set exactly on the lower end of the inclined rails – a midget aircraft actually in position for launching.

'Late through that night I worked feverishly with Kendall to trace back the history of the "Peenemünde Airfield Site". We found that the first experimental ramp had been built late in 1942, during the interval between the earliest two covers of the area. Kendall himself measured and analyzed the ramp and then started drafting an immediate report.

'But the ramp near the airfield was not the only one on the Baltic coast that was reported by Medmenham on 1 December 1943. John Merifield's sorties had brought another piece of exciting news as well. The Air Ministry had asked for photographs of the suspected radar installation at Zinnowitz because they had heard that a Luftwaffe unit was plotting flying bombs launched from this location. So Claude Wavell, as the top radar interpreter, and Neil Simon and Robert Rowell in the Army Section had been searching the wooded shoreline. And almost at the same moment that I was looking at the earlier cover and asking myself what on earth the ramp near the airfield could be, they had found, between Zinnowitz and the village of Kempin, eight miles away down the coast of Usedom, a launching site with firing points aiming out to sea, which also matched up with the foundations for ramps at the ski sites. It was, in fact, a Luftwaffe centre for training the personnel who were going to operate the launching sites in France.

'Before daylight next morning Kendall's report on both Peenemünde and Zinnowitz was on its way to London, with the news that the nature of the most imminent cross-channel threat was at last established beyond doubt. It was going to be a flying bomb.

'Crossbow! The code word superseded Bodyline once it was known for certain that the flying bomb – the V1 – was the danger to be countered first. At this point it seemed that the V1 attacks, when they came, might be of an appalling magnitude. The ski buildings provided storage space for twenty flying tombs at each site, and as there were nearly a hundred sites it seemed possible that the target for launchings was something like 2,000 flying bombs in each 24 hours.

'When was this deluge of flying bombs supposed to begin? That was the next question, and Kendall and the Army interpreters and been busy working out the answer even before it was asked. So many sites had been photographed in France that the average time needed for the early stages of construction could be calculated very accurately, and the photographs of Peenemünde and Zinnowitz helped to fill in the rest of the story. Kendall discussed technical problems with several interpreters who were peacetime architects, and finally came out with an estimate that the minimum time for construction of a ski site was 120 days from start to finish. So the target date for the beginning of the attack might be about six weeks ahead.

'The ski sites had obviously got to be bombed, and at once Medmenham embarked on the huge job of providing material for targeting. Kendall also invented a method of assessing the readiness of each site, so that attacks could be timed for the moment when construction was far advanced but not too dangerously near completion. He worked out a "points system", allocating 100 points to each site, and a certain number to each individual building. Then new cover came in, the interpreters assessed the readiness of each building in points, and their total represented the percentage of readiness of the whole site.

'But at the end of December 1943, when the Allied air forces really let fly at the ski sites, the heavy bombers of the Eighth Air Force were brought in with devastating effect – every site was flattened, whether it was nearly ready or not. Soon the whole system of ski sites was a shambles. The first round of the battle against the flying bomb was an overwhelming victory for the Allies.

'When the bombing of the ski sites first began, the Germans had tried frantically to repair all the damage. But as the attacks grew heavier the policy seemed to change and repair work was concentrated on the firing point and the square building. "So those must be the real essentials," thought Kendall, as he saw this happening at site after site.

'The elaborate storage "skis" and certain other buildings at the sites were not essential to the actual launching, although they would have been essential to the really heavy bombardment that the Germans originally planned.

'At the end of April 1944 – little more than a month before D-Day – Robert Rowell was examining a new cover of the Cherbourg peninsula when he suddenly gasped. Near a village called Belhamelin something peculiar had been constructed between two far buildings. It could be ... yes it must be ... Yes, it was a long concrete platform with pairs of studs embedded in it. Ah! The beginnings of a firing point. And some way from it, in a field, was a heavily camouflaged square building. The two essential installations! It was a launching site of a new, much simpler variety, and the camouflage and dispersal was extremely subtle. The Germans had evidently learnt their lesson over the ski sites, and had made new plans with Allied interpreters as well as Allied bombing in mind. The new sites were horribly difficult to spot, but within a few days twelve had been identified.

'These finds sounded off a new Crossbow alarm, and for the fourth time a special flying programme was laid on. The whole area within 150 miles of London, Southampton and Plymouth was to be photographed yet again. At Medmenham, Kendall put fifteen more interpreters on to Crossbow work.

'By the beginning of June sixty-eight "modified sites" had been founded, most of them oriented to the "London line". But one rather puzzling thing came to light. Once the concrete bases for the ramp and the square building were laid, nothing more happened. Could there be a hold up somewhere? No. It was according to plan that the modified sites were left unfinished. The answer to this was found not in France but at the V1 training centre at Zinnowitz.

'New cover showed that an additional launching site, of the modified type, was being completed there. So Kendall and Rowell were able to observe the manner in which one of these sites was made ready for use. Sections of rail six metres long were brought to the site, and there they were fitted together and erected; while prefabricated parts for the square building were also assembled on the spot.

'The very day before D-Day Kendall broke this news to a Crossbow meeting in London. Its grave implication was, of course, that the modified sites in France, and also perhaps some of the ski sites which had seemed to be abandoned, could be made ready for use within a matter of forty-eight hours. The first warning would be the arrival of components for the ramp and the square building. It was therefore agreed that if this were seen, a signal should immediately be sent to the Air Ministry with the code word Diver.

'During the first few days after the Normandy landings, Crossbow priorities counted for nothing in the reconnaissance programme. "We'll just have to make do as best we can with chance covers of the sites," said Kendall to Rowell, "but we must brief all the interpreters very carefully, and tell them how vitally important it is to spot any components."

'By 11 June there were special Crossbow sorties again, and late that evening photographs of nine of the sites, which had not been covered since D-Day, were brought to Kendall. He took one look at them and sent off the Diver signal. It was in the early hours of the morning of 13 June that the first V1 landed in Britain.

'During the hectic weeks and months that led up to the sending of the Diver signal, the attempt to solve the mystery of the other secret weapon – the V2 rocket – had of necessity taken second place. But a few new clues had been found. In March 1944 a report had reached London that the Germans were making rocket trials at a place called Blizna in the wilds of southeast Poland. Could Blizna be photographed to confirm or disprove the report? Yes, it could. Blizna was 1,000 miles from Benson, right across Germany, but only 600 from San Severo, the photographic reconnaissance base in Italy. So on 15 April a Mosquito from Italy set off for Poland, and far above the forests and marshes between the Vistula and the San photographs were taken of the clearing where the rocket launching had been reported.

'Back at Medmenham Kendall and the Army interpreters pored over the photographs – the place smelt of Crossbow, but there were no rockets to be seen, and none of the big earthworks as at Peenemünde. When Blizna was covered a second time, however, on 5 May, a rocket happened to be in the open. And by comparing the photographs of Blizna with those of Peenemünde it could be established that the rockets had four fins, and that the huge trailers used for moving them were of a special design. This tied up with ground reports of special road vehicles known as Meillerwagen.

'Such scraps of evidence were very valuable, but they could do little to clarify the strongly differing view of the various authorities in London as to how the rocket worked and how it was launched. There was still no agreement when, towards the end of July, amid the stuttering of approaching V1s, the War Cabinet began to be seriously concerned about the possibility of imminent rocket attack. The whole investigation was once again charged with high urgency. It was a challenge to Medmenham.

'Kendall decided that the only thing was to go back over all the previous covers of Peenemünde. Many of them had been interpreted at an early stage of the secret weapon investigation, at a time when the most dominant theories insisted on a huge rocket that could not be launched vertically and could be moved only by rail. Now there were a number of reports of vertical launching and the evidence of the old photographs might appear in quite a fresh light.

'Kendall made his way to the long narrow room where the Crossbow interpreters worked, and sought out Robert Rowell. They agreed to tackle the huge job, which would mean re-examining thirty-five sorties. Evening after evening Kendall returned to the task. Stooped low over the photographs, he would often remain motionless for minutes at a time. One of the best interpreters at Medmenhan once said, "I don't look for things; I let the photographs speak to me," and that was Kendall's approach. Gradually the old photographs began to tell a startling new story.

'He re-examined the great earthworks that dominated the scene, but then his attention focused on the fan-shaped stretch of foreshore that lay to seaward. At the end of the short road from the elliptical earthwork it looked almost as bleakly bare as a parade ground. He checked it patiently from cover to cover, and then at last sat back.

'"Yes, it's asphalt," he said to Rowell. "I've found when they started laying it. The Germans wouldn't lay all that asphalt without good reason." He returned to his stereoscope. Then after a minute or two he handed a pair of prints to Rowell. "This is the 'column 40 feet high' which was photographed last June. Have a look and see what you make of it."

'Rowell looked, and then gave an explosive laugh.

'"A column 40 feet high my foot! It's a rocket sitting on its fins!"

'Kendall smiled and nodded. "That's why they needed the asphalt. The fan-shaped foreshore must be a practice site for operational launchings. The elliptical earthwork was for the early experiments."

'He bent down once more over his stereoscope.

'"So that really is the end of the theory that the launching sites have to be rail served," he went on, looking searchingly at the stretch of asphalt. It was innocent of anything resembling a railway line. "And the only signs of an operational launching site will be a bit of concrete or asphalt."

'"They wouldn't even have to bother with that, would they?" he said. "A bit of any main road would do just as well."

'From 8 September 1944, when the first V2 was launched against England, throughout the months during which the "drizzle of rockets" continued, innumerable sorties were flown to pinpoints that had been reported as launching sites, and the interpreters searched thousands upon thousands of photographs. But in only two cases – where clearings in woods were found at the suspected spots – could any suspicious signs be reported, not one single operational launching site was found. In fact they did not exist. As General Dornberger explains in his book V2 the rocket could be launched from "a bit of planking on a forest track, or the overgrown track itself". The only hope of spotting a V2 launching site was if a photographic aircraft happened to pass overhead when a rocket was set upright being fuelled. Otherwise there was virtually nothing to see, for the Meillerwagen were easily concealed under trees. It was a one-in-a-million chance, and even if it occurred it would not provide a target for attack, as the "sites" were completely mobile. Nevertheless, the frustrating search had to go on.

'Such impotence, such lagging far behind reports from other sources, was something quite new for photographic intelligence. The ground reports were very emphatic at this time, as one might expect. To the residents of The Hague, the thunderous roar of rockets made it only too clear that the Haagsche Bosch was the main launching area. Eventually, it was on photographs of The Hague that operational rockets were first found by the interpreters. On 29 December there were thirteen of them, "concealed" under the trees in The Hague's main park. Evidently this was a forward storage point as well as a launching area.

'During the first weeks of the New Year, however, the Allied attacks on the Haagsche Bosch succeeded in driving the Germans out of it, and London had a brief respite from V2s. But then the rockets started coming over again. Where were they coming from?

'On the afternoon of 26 February 1945, Flight Lieutenant George Reynolds, one of the day shift of Crossbow interpreters, picked up a sortie box and opened the plot. It was new cover of The Hague. "Jolly good quality," thought Reynolds, as he glanced through the stack of photographs, and he felt sorry that he was just due to hand over to the new shift. "But I'll just have time to start looking through it," he thought. He began working through the sortie and then suddenly called across the room to Rowell: "Robert! Quick! Come and look at this."

'The million-to-one chance had come off. There it was, clear as you like: a V2 rocket sitting on its fins, with fuelling vehicles clustered round. So this was the new launching area: Duindigt racecourse in the northeast suburbs of The Hague. Could it be a storage area too? But the Germans were managing to dispense with forward storage points altogether. During the following month, until the V2 attacks ended on 27 March 1945, only an occasional rocket on a Meillerwagen was to be seen.

'If Hitler's ideas of sticking to massive concrete "launching shelter" had prevailed, the tale would have been very different. There would have been something to bite on. But the plain fact of the matter is that General Dornberger's almost ridiculously simple conception of how the V2s should be launched defeated Allied photographic reconnaissance.

Chapter 10

The WAAF Abroad

The WAAF went overseas, though not in great numbers. Fewer than 9,000 girls, or 4.5 per cent of the total strength, actually served abroad, but this small proportion was in no way due to lack of volunteers. The official view was that problems must be involved in posting girls abroad, and it could only be agreed to when the shortage of manpower made it essential. The girls were not to be merely morale boosters for the RAF!

Throughout the war the question of tropical kit remained under constant discussion: its style, quantity and quality. Officers who went to the USA in 1940 wore plain clothes until America joined the war. Then they had khaki gabardine tunics and skirts made locally to the official pattern. Girls going to Egypt in 1941 also tended to buy their uniforms locally and to make their own regulation about wearing it. In 1942 the powers in London decreed that a summer dress would be an improvement on the khaki tunic, which was superseded by a loose jacket. The officers in North America continued to wear the gabardine tunic and skirt, with silk stockings and RAF fore-and-aft cap, while those in Egypt adapted the uniform to their own tastes. The uniform dress proved very unpopular and fell entirely out of use!

Airwomen sent to the Middle East were also confronted with kit problems, for they were expected to wear khaki drill similar to the ATS. The WAAF had been used to blue and found khaki a depressing colour. The stock of cotton goods of any kind was so low in Britain, however, that little could be done to meet the girls' wishes. The official view remained that in all places throughout the world they should wear the same tropical kit. Discussions were still proceeding on this vexed point to women into the spring of 1945. The WAAFS felt that even an open-necked shirt and a khaki skirt were neither cool nor pleasant enough for the hot season in such areas as south-east Asia. It was not until after the war was over, however, that agreement became possible to allow girls to have two dresses made locally of airman's shirting, and that silk stockings and neat black sandals were permissible.

There were similar woes over officers' kit allowance. The figure for the purchase of tropical kit stood at precisely £5 – hardly enough for the tin trunk needed! This amount was very reluctantly raised to £10 in 1943 but a request for £26 was rejected. Only after the whole question had been bandied about for years was a further increase granted. Miss Irene Ward, MP, raised the matter in the House of Commons and continued to do so till at last an increase was made to £22 10s – actually after VE-Day!

Among all the arrangements necessary before WAAFs could be sent abroad, were the regulations for possible pregnancy. It was settled that in any cases of unmarried pregnancy, the woman should be returned to Britain as soon as possible, those for the Middle East to travel by sea up to four months and by air up to six months. Then welfare arrangements would be available similar to those for girls serving at home. But in fact no girl gave birth to a child overseas during the war.

The first overseas posting of all consisted of three cypher officers to New York in July 1940. These lucky assistant section officers went at the request of the Ministry of Aircraft Production to the office of the Consul General in New York, to handle the typex cypher traffic for the British Air Commission. The contrast could hardly have been greater: from a Britain-all-alone to an America still at peace.

The following March, a similar section was posted to New York for duties with the British Purchasing Commission of the Ministry of Supply. All these girls went on to Washington, where in June 1941 the RAF Delegation was formed. When America entered the war, this branch naturally increased rapidly and combined into the RAF

Delegation cypher section. In July 1942 the Directorate of Equipment at the Delegation moved to Dayton, Ohio, and a WAAF section was set up there.

The Delegation cypher office establishment went ahead by leaps to meet the traffic, which averaged about 60,000 groups per day, with peaks up to 90,000 groups in the Delegation office alone. By February 1944 the total WAAF force covering all the cypher sections controlled by the RAF Delegation amounted to a squadron officer, 7 flight officers and 47 section officers. While they were serving in the USA, not surprisingly seven girls married America citizens and a further six married Canadians, but in October 1944 it was ruled that WAAF officers married to American citizens could no longer continue to carry out cypher duties.

Throughout the war, accommodation in New York and Washington was hard to find, and most hotels in Washington would accept visitors for only five days. After that time, officers were expected to have found their own place to live. Most shared apartments or houses, while a few lived in furnished rooms or with American families. Several apartments were occupied by a succession of WAAF officers for anything up to five years.

The normal tour of duty in the USA was two years. After the summer of 1942, the code and cypher officers spent five months of their tour at one of the outstations, either New York, Dayton, or another new one opened, Nassau. Postings to these outstations from Washington were strictly by roster, but officers could ballot for which one was preferred. Needless to say, New York and Nassau got more votes than Dayton!

The Bahamas unit was equally vital, but had the extra asset of serving as a comparative rest cure for the WAAFs from the hectic pace of work in the capital. The island offered a wonderful chance of sailing, swimming, golf, tennis and generally participating in a social setup, which even in 1943–1945 was whirling pretty fast.

The remaining region where WAAF officers found themselves on the North American continent was above the forty-ninth parallel. In 1941, the headquarters of Ferry Command had been formed in Montreal and a few RAF and WAAF officers were working there on codes and cyphers. By the middle of 1945, no fewer than 70 lucky WAAFs were serving in the newly created No 45 Group. They worked not only at Montreal and its airport of Dorval, but also in Bermuda, at Gander and Botwood in Newfoundland, Goose Bay in Labrador, and back across the American border at Elizabeth City in North Carolina and San Diego, California. And even Trinidad. The weather varied violently between one station and another. One month officers might be enduring the complete isolation, bitter cold, wild weather and the dehydrated food of Gander or Goose Bay, and then they might suddenly find themselves in the glamour of Bermuda or the Bahamas, for Nassau was yet another station of Ferry Command.

Gander was actually the second outstation to have WAAFs, the first half dozen officers arriving in May 1942, and despite the hard climate, it remained one of the most popular places. The temperature ranges from 50–65 degrees in the very short summer down to 10 degrees in winter, with blizzards and driving snow reaching 90 mph. At times like these, the sense of isolation was complete, since all travel ceased– there was no post and even radio faded out. Nor did ferry pilots try to fly through the Newfoundland blizzards.

The girls lived in an old Rangers hut, which was later transported bodily on to a brick foundation. It had one of the only two baths in Gander! It was also equipped with a refrigerator, electric cooker and central heating, which frequently failed and had to be supplemented by a stove. The domestic staff was inexperienced local men, and for the first two years, the food was poor and badly cooked. Later on the quality improved by the institution of a weekly air service carrying fresh foods, while a civilian Swedish–Canadian chef raised the standard of the cuisine. The WAAF officers were also called on to entertain the many distinguished travellers who arrived almost daily from flights held up or merely stopping for a short time at Gander. While here, the girls received a special allowance of one Canadian dollar a day, but the cost of living was practically nil, since food was free, cigarettes cheap, and the local lumberjacks' store offered no incentive for spending sprees.

Nassau provided the utter opposite. Here the airfields site was swampy and infested with mosquitoes, and unsuitable for the WAAFs. So they rented a house on the seashore, large, airy and well furnished. But it should be borne in mind that they worked hard wherever they were, whether clad in tropical kit or sub-Arctic attire, all of which they had to find locally. The government was still studying exactly what sort of kit they needed.

It was to the Middle East, however, that the bulk of the overseas WAAFs were sent. As in England, all cypher work out there had been done originally by civilian women, mostly officers' wives. WAAFs were suggested for the job late in 1940, and the first draft sailed from England the next summer. An idea of the difficulty of transport in wartime can be got from the route and time taken for these girls to get to Cairo: they had to make a long journey by sea to Freetown and Lagos and then proceed by air to Egypt, arriving in early September. They were posted to Cairo, Alexandria, Jerusalem and Ismailia. Then numbers gradually rose to some 200 WAAF officers by the end of 1942.

Outstanding among the entire number of WAAF officers serving in this theatre were those attached to Telecommunications, Middle East. This was built in the desert, just beyond Heliopolis, to take the signals and cypher sections of Headquarters, RAF Middle East, to receive and despatch all traffic for the ME headquarters, and to act as a link in the worldwide network of wireless contacts.

The job done by TME, as it was known, was excellent, but the working conditions could not be described in the same way. The W/T station itself, with its traffic office, high speed and teleprinter rooms, and cypher department, was specifically designed for its function, and yet, being underground and fitted with an air-conditioning plant that was more often than not out of order, it got stuffy and sometimes stiflingly hot. The noise of the machines was nerve racking, and after six hours of it, the girls emerged feeling mentally and physically exhausted. Sickness became inevitable, but the WAAF stuck it for eighteen months before handing over to the RAF.

Due to climatic and other factors, it was decided to limit the trades of airwomen abroad to the sedentary or clerical kind, such as clerks, nursing orderlies, dental clerk orderlies and so on. These were to be obtained by training a locally enlisted force, composed of Palestinians, Greeks and other Allied nationals. The plan proved only partially successful, though, with the enrolment of some 800 girls. Deficiencies still existed and so the Air Ministry agreed to send out 2,000 airwomen in four drafts of 500. These girls eventually served in Egypt, the Levant, Cyprus, East Africa, Aden, Syria and Iraq.

In June 1943 WAAF cypher officers were suddenly needed at Algiers to help headquarters, Mediterranean Air Command, with the heavy cypher traffic being handled by RAF officers. This was a direct reflection of the rapidly rising tempo of operations in this theatre, with July destined as the month for the invasion of Sicily.

At first the WAAFs had to put up with trying conditions. They had a villa, a mile and a half from the headquarters, which was literally surrounded by troops of every nationality except British! Moreover, the villa was virtually unfurnished, with no glass in the windows and no hot water. Neither had they a mess, so took meals in the Junior American Officers' Mess. Not that that sounds too much of an ordeal!

In February 1944 all the WAAF officers moved up to Tunis, where they enjoyed a month of comparative luxury before being flown to Italy with MAAF Headquarters. Here they were housed in a big Italian villa, and they were crowded, cold and short of hot water. Messing was far from good, and laundry, hairdressing and replacement of kit all proved awkward. But to offset these disadvantages, they had the enviable thrill of being a mere thirty miles from the front line of the Italian battle zone. They kept very cheerful and accepted lack of sleep and leave as naturally as airmen on active service. The war gradually moved northwards, and Caserta, their base, became a rear headquarters. Airwomen joined the officers in more general duties there and at Algiers, and the total number serving with MAAF reached 84 officers and 1,004 airwomen.

While the war in the Mediterranean was proceeding to plan, or as near as it ever could, the WAAF were getting ready for the invasion from the north. D-Day, 6 June. The question of WAAFs serving on the Continent had been discussed for a very long time, and in December 1943 the Air Ministry ruled that none should go there until conditions could be investigated: except of course the SOE officers, several of whom were already there. So the WAAFs were to remain with the Second Tactical Air Force or the Allied Expeditionary Force Headquarters, which were both busily preparing in Britain.

In the New Year, however, the Air Ministry authorized the formation of a WAAF section, and were approached for permission to take these women with the Headquarters when it moved overseas. Late in May, Whitehall finally agreed to allow WAAF personnel across the Channel under these conditions. All were to be volunteers; officers to be 23 or over and without domestic ties; airwomen to be over 21, single, married without children, or with children over 14.

Some special women were allowed across soon after D-Day, but generally it was not until 3 August 1944, when a WAAF staff officer had found suitable housing at Le Touquet, that the first party of one officer and four airwomen went to France on 5 August. Small parties followed until there were about 100 by mid-September.

Drafting to the Continent went ahead slowly. By the end of the year, only 260 airwomen were in France, not for lack of the volunteers but because the German breakthrough in the Ardennes put a temporary stop to posting. As the situation at the front improved, 500 more girls went across, and by March they were serving in 25 RAF units in France and Belgium. On 6 April, two officers and eight airwomen moved up to Suchteln from Brussels with the Second Tactical Air Force, and so became the first WAAF to be stationed in Germany itself. Before VE-Day more than 100 officers and 1,500 airwomen were in Western Europe altogether. So popular was this duty that in the few cases of indiscipline occurring, the worst punishment, which could be inflicted or threatened, was to return the offender to Britain. The fact that this was done in one or two cases acted as a marked deterrent to any other girls, and behaviour was all the better because of it.

So VE-Day came and went, but the WAAF were to go still further abroad than Europe, the Mediterranean and the Middle East. They had a positive part awaiting them in the final stages of the Far East war.

During 1943 the shortage of manpower in the Air Command of South-East Asia grew so serious that the RAF decided to review the chances of employing the WAAF in India and Ceylon. The shortages became so acute the next year as to imperil the actual future operations to which the RAF was committed, on 29 June 1944, therefore the Air Commander in Chief asked the Air Ministry for 185 WAAF officers and 1,375 airwomen to serve in Delhi, Bombay and units in Ceylon. He also felt that the arrival of airwomen would help raise the morale of the men, many of who had been out there for a long time.

The request received approval and the first draft of 250 WAAFs reached Bombay by sea on 9 November 1944. Two special trains took them up to Delhi, where a camp had been completed for them only the previous day! A second draft sailed into Colombo on 11 January, and other small drafts continued to come until May.

The WAAF served in their usual variety of ways throughout the Indian Command. In March 1945, a WAAF section consisting mainly of nursing orderlies for No 10 RAF Hospital was opened in Karachi, but though nursing orderlies were also equally needed for No 9 Hospital at Calcutta, suitable quarters for the girls just could not be found there. A WAAF section was hurriedly opened at the port of Trincomalèe, early in 1945, to assist Operation Dracula, the assault on Rangoon. They did good work and stayed open until the operation had been successfully completed.

Meanwhile other WAAFs from Coastal and Fighter Commands were carrying on their jobs in the Battle of the Indian Ocean, one typical contingent of them working at a Ceylon flying boat base. As the aircraft came in to land on an airstrip on the coast of the island, they veered into view from a strange type of control tower, mounted on bamboo poles and built of dried grass. After clambering up a lot of steps and a perilous ladder, WAAF radiotelephone operators reached their duty post. From the tower balcony they could see, spread out below them, a hinterland of palm trees and forests ... the landing strip ... the dotted buildings of the camp. On one side lay the sea; on the other a blue lagoon with little islands and buoys, where the great flying boats swept in to rest after their intercontinental trips.

A Sunderland was in the offing, and an airwoman with headphones on spoke to it. 'Are you receiving?' She gave the strength of reception.

'Coming in to land in five minutes.'

The WAAF made sure that the way was clear. 'OK.'

In a few minutes, the pilot spoke to her again. 'In circuit. May we pancake?'

'You may pancake.'

Like a huge white flying fish, the Sunderland glided smoothly on to the surface of the water, and reported, 'We are now waterborne.'

The WAAF gave the number of the buoy that the boat must use, and received the acknowledgment: 'Moored up. Thanks.'

The R/T operator on duty, LACW Aida Smith, of Glasgow, felt rather like a London policeman at a traffic centre. But the big lagoon could hardly have been further from the capital. The Sunderlands and Catalinas took off for anti-submarine sweeps and shipping escort duties, and others landed after the long haul from Australia. Corporal Sylvia Munroe, of Alton, Hants, who also worked in Flying Control, gradually got to realize that the Indian Ocean is 23 times the size of the North Sea.

In the ops room itself, Sergeant S Elton, of Wimborne, Dorset, a Coastal Command plotter, worked at wall maps where the Battle of the Indian Ocean were set out – and fought out. These girls, just as they shared secrets at home, knew the whereabouts of patrolling aircraft and Allied shipping, and the suspected positions of any hostile submarines or ships. They prepared the 'gen' wallets for aircrews and gave them their cartridges and recognition signals. Next door, in the intelligence room, a WAAF clerk, LACW Mary Coley, of Kinkley, Leicestershire, was helping the intelligence officer to keep the display of graphs and maps up to date.

Elsewhere round the camp, in a hut under the coconut trees,

WAAF equipment assistants were at work with the various flying boat spares they handled; WAAF clerks were busy at headquarters; and WAAFs manned the telephones. Off duty they swam in a pool scooped out of coral and sunbathed on a palm beach. But on duty their job helped to keep the Indian Ocean safe for Allied ships and planes.

Other WAAFs went over that ocean to conquer fresh fields further east: to Singapore and Hong Kong. But by that time, the war was over, the victory won.

The original object of the WAAF was to keep the aircraft of the Royal Air Force flying; to ensure that no machine was ever grounded because men were employed on duties that could be done by women. At the outbreak of war, the WAAF numbered fewer than 2,000 airwomen, in 6 trades and an officer branch – untrained and inexperienced.

The service steadily increased, both in numbers and efficiency, becoming more and more vital as the manpower shortage worsened. At the peak of the WAAF in mid-1943, nearly 182,000 women were serving in 22 officer branches and 75 trades. Without the WAAF, the RAF would have needed 150,000 more men, who could only have been found at the expense of the other services or industry. So the WAAF won the war, just as much as the men of the RAF.

Appendix

AWARDS

GC
A/S/O (Flight Officer) Joan DM Pearson
Assistant Section Officer Noor Inayat Khan

DBE
Air Chief Commandant Katherine Trefusis Forbes

CBE
Group Officer Isobel Mary Campbell
Group Officer Selena Frances Wynne-Eaton

OBE
Group Officer Elspeth Barrie
Squadron Officer Diana Mary Barton
Squadron Officer Alice Winifred Patience Bruzaud
Wing Officer (Group Officer) Lilian Marguerite Crowther
Squadron Officer Mary Hibbert
Group Officer Cecily Mary McAlery
Squadron Officer Margaret McManus
Squadron Officer Louise Hilliard Rankin
Squadron Officer M Ryley
Squadron Officer Joan Anne Williams
Squadron Officer Margaret Wallace Wright Ford

MBE
Flight Officer Constance Babington Smith
Squadron Officer Lady Dorothy Bowhill
Flight Officer Joan Bradbury
Flight Officer Betty Rose Bradford
Squadron Officer Mildred Georgia Breedon
Flight Officer Margaret Cleater
Flight Officer Jane Stuart Clother
Squadron Officer Catherine Elizabeth Clough
Flight Officer Constance Marion Colbeck Davies
Flight Officer IR Cryer
Flight Officer Agnes Emily Davies
Flight Officer Nellie N Evans
Flight Officer Lady Elizabeth Freeman
A/S/O (GO) Felicity H Hanbury
Flight Officer Anne Scot Henderson
Flight Officer Mary Hodgson
Flight Officer Pearl Gwendolin Hollick
Flight Officer (WO) Magdalene FM Holloway
Flight Officer Gladys Mary Hume
Flight Officer Margaret Caroline Marks
Warrant Officer Constance McLaughlin
Flight Officer Betty Dorothea Moore
Section Officer Aileen Bowen Morris
Flight Officer (SO) Margaret Mary Mortimer
Flight Officer Helen Murdoch-Grant
Section Officer Violet Mary Oliver
Flight Officer Barbara Pemberton
Flight Officer Peggy Potter (née Purnell)
Flight Officer AL Rundle
Flight Officer Gladys Mary Shadbolt
Section Officer Joan Hilda Swain
Flight Officer Stella Roy Taylor
Flight Officer Anne Beatrice Walker
Squadron Officer Norah Louise McNeil Warren
Flight Officer MBK Wherry
Section Officer Joyce Wood
Wing Officer Frances Agnes Joynson Wreford

MM
Corporal (Flight Sergeant) Joan Avis Hearn
Corporal (FO) Elspeth C Henderson
Sergeant Joan E Mortimer
Corporal (Warrant Officer) Josephine M Robins
Sergeant Helen E Turner

Sergeant (Section Officer) Jean L Youle

BEM
Corporal Olive Joan Annetts
Sergeant Mary Bayliss
Flight Sergeant Enid Bertrand (née Vaughan)
Corporal Mary Blake
Flight Sergeant Lydia Betty Bonser
Leading ACW PM Budd
Sergeant Florence Celeste
Leading ACW Ruby Churchill
Flight Sergeant Daphnes Clay
Leading ACW Ivy Cross
Flight Sergeant Kathleen Downe
Leading ACW Lilian Sarah Ellis
Flight Sergeant Alice Edith Ferris
Flight Sergeant EFA France
Sergeant Flora Dorothy Hands
Corporal Pamela Margerite Hanford
Flight Sergeant Margery Lorna Hessom
Sergeant Betsy Holloway
Corporal Alice Horton (née Holden)
Sergeant Edith Irene Dora Hosscrop
Leading ACW Barbara MI Jones
Corporal Pamela Doria Lester Sidebotham
Sergeant Sheila Marjorie Lockett (née Wear)
Sergeant Phyllis Margery Lockwood
Sergeant Christina Junette Margaret Mackay
Sergeant Dorothy Iris Martin
Corporal Elsie Margaret Mawson
Corporal Jessie Glennie McKean
Leading ACW Kathleen Lucy McKinlay
Flight Sergeant Ivy Lilian Millet
Corporal Doris Mary Mothersole
Leading ACW Doris Margaret Nichol
Sergeant Mary Isobel Royd
Flight Sergeant Laura Evelin Rutt
Flight Sergeant Jessie Mary Shannon
Flight Sergeant NM Shepherd
Flight Sergeant Monica Shezall

Corporal Janet Smith
Corporal Joan Pauline Stoneham
Corporal Hilda Marjorie Terry
Sergeant Florence May Watson
Sergeant Ellen Beatrice Webster

Commended for Brave Conduct
ACW Margaret Hay McBurnie
Corporal JM Standing

USA Legion of Merit
Leading ACW Isobella Greig Leask

Special Operations Executive
Yolande Elsa Maria Beekman (née Unternahrer), Croix de Guerre Flight Officer Muriel Tamara Byck, Mention in Despatches Jeanne Therese de Vibraye Baseden (Mrs Bailey), MBE Section Officer
Acting Section Officer Sonia Esmee Florence Butt (Mrs d'Artois), MBE Assistant Section
Flight Officer Beatrice Yvonne Cormeau, MBE, Croix de Guerre
Flight Officer Cecile Pearl Cornioley (née Witherington), MBE, Croix de Guerre
Christine Granville (née Countess Skarbek), GM, OBE, Croix de Guerre
Assistant Section Officer Noor Inayat Khan
Section Officer Phyllis Ada Latour, MBE
Section Officer Cecily Margot Lefort, Recommended for MBE
Section Officer Maureen Patricia O'Sullivan (Mrs Alvey), MBE
Assistant Section Officer Lilian Verna Rolfe, Mentioned in Despatches
Section Officer Diana Hope Rowden, Mentioned in Despatches
Section Officer Anne Marie Walters (Mme Comert), MBE